Forensic Science: A Very Short Introduction

Praise for the first edition

Perfect corrective for all CSI Scunthorpe wannabes. This
no-nonsense guide is an admirable alternative to the CSI science
fiction juggernaut. Jim Fraser discusses expert evidence, DNA,
fingerprints and confirmation bias...Fascinating.

Fortean Times

Does exactly what it says on the tin, with clarity, authority, and élan.

Paul Roberts, Professor of Criminal Jurisprudence

He...provides a clear and exciting glimpse into the world of
forensic science as a realm of complex activity at the interface of
science and law. The reader is held spellbound by references to
famous criminal cases in British legal history as well as to
popular movies such as Quentin Tarantino's 'Pulp Fiction'. The
book is enjoyable and delightful to read, and the topics can
easily be grasped and appreciated even by non-expert readers.

Journal of Forensic Medicine and Pathology

VERY SHORT INTRODUCTIONS are for anyone wanting a stimulating and accessible way into a new subject. They are written by experts, and have been translated into more than 45 different languages.

The series began in 1995, and now covers a wide variety of topics in every discipline. The VSI library currently contains over 600 volumes—a Very Short Introduction to everything from Psychology and Philosophy of Science to American History and Relativity—and continues to grow in every subject area.

Very Short Introductions available now:

ABOLITIONISM Richard S. Newman
THE ABRAHAMIC RELIGIONS
    Charles L. Cohen
ACCOUNTING Christopher Nobes
ADAM SMITH Christopher J. Berry
ADOLESCENCE Peter K. Smith
ADVERTISING Winston Fletcher
AERIAL WARFARE Frank Ledwidge
AESTHETICS Bence Nanay
AFRICAN AMERICAN RELIGION
    Eddie S. Glaude Jr
AFRICAN HISTORY
    John Parker and Richard Rathbone
AFRICAN POLITICS Ian Taylor
AFRICAN RELIGIONS
    Jacob K. Olupona
AGEING Nancy A. Pachana
AGNOSTICISM Robin Le Poidevin
AGRICULTURE Paul Brassley and
    Richard Soffe
ALBERT CAMUS Oliver Gloag
ALEXANDER THE GREAT
    Hugh Bowden
ALGEBRA Peter M. Higgins
AMERICAN CULTURAL HISTORY
    Eric Avila
AMERICAN FOREIGN RELATIONS
    Andrew Preston
AMERICAN HISTORY Paul S. Boyer
AMERICAN IMMIGRATION
    David A. Gerber
AMERICAN LEGAL HISTORY
    G. Edward White
AMERICAN NAVAL HISTORY
    Craig L. Symonds

AMERICAN POLITICAL HISTORY
    Donald Critchlow
AMERICAN POLITICAL PARTIES
    AND ELECTIONS L. Sandy Maisel
AMERICAN POLITICS
    Richard M. Valelly
THE AMERICAN PRESIDENCY
    Charles O. Jones
THE AMERICAN REVOLUTION
    Robert J. Allison
AMERICAN SLAVERY
    Heather Andrea Williams
THE AMERICAN WEST Stephen Aron
AMERICAN WOMEN'S HISTORY
    Susan Ware
ANAESTHESIA Aidan O'Donnell
ANALYTIC PHILOSOPHY
    Michael Beaney
ANARCHISM Colin Ward
ANCIENT ASSYRIA Karen Radner
ANCIENT EGYPT Ian Shaw
ANCIENT EGYPTIAN ART AND
    ARCHITECTURE Christina Riggs
ANCIENT GREECE Paul Cartledge
THE ANCIENT NEAR EAST
    Amanda H. Podany
ANCIENT PHILOSOPHY Julia Annas
ANCIENT WARFARE Harry Sidebottom
ANGELS David Albert Jones
ANGLICANISM Mark Chapman
THE ANGLO-SAXON AGE John Blair
ANIMAL BEHAVIOUR
    Tristram D. Wyatt
THE ANIMAL KINGDOM
    Peter Holland

ANIMAL RIGHTS David DeGrazia
THE ANTARCTIC Klaus Dodds
ANTHROPOCENE Erle C. Ellis
ANTISEMITISM Steven Beller
ANXIETY Daniel Freeman and
   Jason Freeman
THE APOCRYPHAL GOSPELS
   Paul Foster
APPLIED MATHEMATICS Alain Goriely
ARCHAEOLOGY Paul Bahn
ARCHITECTURE Andrew Ballantyne
ARISTOCRACY William Doyle
ARISTOTLE Jonathan Barnes
ART HISTORY Dana Arnold
ART THEORY Cynthia Freeland
ARTIFICIAL INTELLIGENCE
   Margaret A. Boden
ASIAN AMERICAN HISTORY
   Madeline Y. Hsu
ASTROBIOLOGY David C. Catling
ASTROPHYSICS James Binney
ATHEISM Julian Baggini
THE ATMOSPHERE Paul I. Palmer
AUGUSTINE Henry Chadwick
AUSTRALIA Kenneth Morgan
AUTISM Uta Frith
AUTOBIOGRAPHY Laura Marcus
THE AVANT GARDE David Cottington
THE AZTECS David Carrasco
BABYLONIA Trevor Bryce
BACTERIA Sebastian G. B. Amyes
BANKING John Goddard and
   John O. S. Wilson
BARTHES Jonathan Culler
THE BEATS David Sterritt
BEAUTY Roger Scruton
BEHAVIOURAL ECONOMICS
   Michelle Baddeley
BESTSELLERS John Sutherland
THE BIBLE John Riches
BIBLICAL ARCHAEOLOGY
   Eric H. Cline
BIG DATA Dawn E. Holmes
BIOGRAPHY Hermione Lee
BIOMETRICS Michael Fairhurst
BLACK HOLES Katherine Blundell
BLOOD Chris Cooper
THE BLUES Elijah Wald
THE BODY Chris Shilling
THE BOOK OF COMMON PRAYER
   Brian Cummings

THE BOOK OF MORMON
   Terryl Givens
BORDERS Alexander C. Diener and
   Joshua Hagen
THE BRAIN Michael O'Shea
BRANDING Robert Jones
THE BRICS Andrew F. Cooper
THE BRITISH CONSTITUTION
   Martin Loughlin
THE BRITISH EMPIRE Ashley Jackson
BRITISH POLITICS Anthony Wright
BUDDHA Michael Carrithers
BUDDHISM Damien Keown
BUDDHIST ETHICS Damien Keown
BYZANTIUM Peter Sarris
C. S. LEWIS James Como
CALVINISM Jon Balserak
CANCER Nicholas James
CAPITALISM James Fulcher
CATHOLICISM Gerald O'Collins
CAUSATION Stephen Mumford and
   Rani Lill Anjum
THE CELL Terence Allen and
   Graham Cowling
THE CELTS Barry Cunliffe
CHAOS Leonard Smith
CHARLES DICKENS Jenny Hartley
CHEMISTRY Peter Atkins
CHILD PSYCHOLOGY Usha Goswami
CHILDREN'S LITERATURE
   Kimberley Reynolds
CHINESE LITERATURE
   Sabina Knight
CHOICE THEORY Michael Allingham
CHRISTIAN ART Beth Williamson
CHRISTIAN ETHICS D. Stephen Long
CHRISTIANITY Linda Woodhead
CIRCADIAN RHYTHMS
   Russell Foster and Leon Kreitzman
CITIZENSHIP Richard Bellamy
CIVIL ENGINEERING
   David Muir Wood
CLASSICAL LITERATURE
   William Allan
CLASSICAL MYTHOLOGY
   Helen Morales
CLASSICS Mary Beard and
   John Henderson
CLAUSEWITZ Michael Howard
CLIMATE Mark Maslin
CLIMATE CHANGE Mark Maslin

CLINICAL PSYCHOLOGY
    Susan Llewelyn and
    Katie Aafjes-van Doorn
COGNITIVE NEUROSCIENCE
    Richard Passingham
THE COLD WAR Robert McMahon
COLONIAL AMERICA Alan Taylor
COLONIAL LATIN AMERICAN
    LITERATURE Rolena Adorno
COMBINATORICS Robin Wilson
COMEDY Matthew Bevis
COMMUNISM Leslie Holmes
COMPARATIVE LITERATURE
    Ben Hutchinson
COMPLEXITY John H. Holland
THE COMPUTER Darrel Ince
COMPUTER SCIENCE
    Subrata Dasgupta
CONCENTRATION CAMPS
    Dan Stone
CONFUCIANISM Daniel K. Gardner
THE CONQUISTADORS
    Matthew Restall and
    Felipe Fernández-Armesto
CONSCIENCE Paul Strohm
CONSCIOUSNESS Susan Blackmore
CONTEMPORARY ART
    Julian Stallabrass
CONTEMPORARY FICTION
    Robert Eaglestone
CONTINENTAL PHILOSOPHY
    Simon Critchley
COPERNICUS Owen Gingerich
CORAL REEFS Charles Sheppard
CORPORATE SOCIAL
    RESPONSIBILITY Jeremy Moon
CORRUPTION Leslie Holmes
COSMOLOGY Peter Coles
COUNTRY MUSIC Richard Carlin
CRIME FICTION Richard Bradford
CRIMINAL JUSTICE Julian V. Roberts
CRIMINOLOGY Tim Newburn
CRITICAL THEORY
    Stephen Eric Bronner
THE CRUSADES Christopher Tyerman
CRYPTOGRAPHY Fred Piper and
    Sean Murphy
CRYSTALLOGRAPHY A. M. Glazer
THE CULTURAL REVOLUTION
    Richard Curt Kraus

DADA AND SURREALISM
    David Hopkins
DANTE Peter Hainsworth and
    David Robey
DARWIN Jonathan Howard
THE DEAD SEA SCROLLS
    Timothy H. Lim
DECADENCE David Weir
DECOLONIZATION Dane Kennedy
DEMOCRACY Bernard Crick
DEMOGRAPHY Sarah Harper
DEPRESSION Jan Scott and
    Mary Jane Tacchi
DERRIDA Simon Glendinning
DESCARTES Tom Sorell
DESERTS Nick Middleton
DESIGN John Heskett
DEVELOPMENT Ian Goldin
DEVELOPMENTAL BIOLOGY
    Lewis Wolpert
THE DEVIL Darren Oldridge
DIASPORA Kevin Kenny
DICTIONARIES Lynda Mugglestone
DINOSAURS David Norman
DIPLOMACY Joseph M. Siracusa
DOCUMENTARY FILM
    Patricia Aufderheide
DREAMING J. Allan Hobson
DRUGS Les Iversen
DRUIDS Barry Cunliffe
DYNASTY Jeroen Duindam
DYSLEXIA Margaret J. Snowling
EARLY MUSIC Thomas Forrest Kelly
THE EARTH Martin Redfern
EARTH SYSTEM SCIENCE
    Tim Lenton
ECONOMICS Partha Dasgupta
EDUCATION Gary Thomas
EGYPTIAN MYTH Geraldine Pinch
EIGHTEENTH-CENTURY BRITAIN
    Paul Langford
THE ELEMENTS Philip Ball
EMOTION Dylan Evans
EMPIRE Stephen Howe
ENERGY SYSTEMS Nick Jenkins
ENGELS Terrell Carver
ENGINEERING David Blockley
THE ENGLISH LANGUAGE
    Simon Horobin
ENGLISH LITERATURE Jonathan Bate

THE ENLIGHTENMENT
  John Robertson
ENTREPRENEURSHIP Paul Westhead
  and Mike Wright
ENVIRONMENTAL ECONOMICS
  Stephen Smith
ENVIRONMENTAL ETHICS
  Robin Attfield
ENVIRONMENTAL LAW
  Elizabeth Fisher
ENVIRONMENTAL POLITICS
  Andrew Dobson
EPICUREANISM Catherine Wilson
EPIDEMIOLOGY Rodolfo Saracci
ETHICS Simon Blackburn
ETHNOMUSICOLOGY Timothy Rice
THE ETRUSCANS Christopher Smith
EUGENICS Philippa Levine
THE EUROPEAN UNION
  Simon Usherwood and John Pinder
EUROPEAN UNION LAW
  Anthony Arnull
EVOLUTION Brian and
  Deborah Charlesworth
EXISTENTIALISM Thomas Flynn
EXPLORATION Stewart A. Weaver
EXTINCTION Paul B. Wignall
THE EYE Michael Land
FAIRY TALE Marina Warner
FAMILY LAW Jonathan Herring
FASCISM Kevin Passmore
FASHION Rebecca Arnold
FEDERALISM Mark J. Rozell and
  Clyde Wilcox
FEMINISM Margaret Walters
FILM Michael Wood
FILM MUSIC Kathryn Kalinak
FILM NOIR James Naremore
THE FIRST WORLD WAR
  Michael Howard
FOLK MUSIC Mark Slobin
FOOD John Krebs
FORENSIC PSYCHOLOGY
  David Canter
FORENSIC SCIENCE Jim Fraser
FORESTS Jaboury Ghazoul
FOSSILS Keith Thomson
FOUCAULT Gary Gutting
THE FOUNDING FATHERS
  R. B. Bernstein

FRACTALS Kenneth Falconer
FREE SPEECH Nigel Warburton
FREE WILL Thomas Pink
FREEMASONRY Andreas Önnerfors
FRENCH LITERATURE John D. Lyons
THE FRENCH REVOLUTION
  William Doyle
FREUD Anthony Storr
FUNDAMENTALISM Malise Ruthven
FUNGI Nicholas P. Money
THE FUTURE Jennifer M. Gidley
GALAXIES John Gribbin
GALILEO Stillman Drake
GAME THEORY Ken Binmore
GANDHI Bhikhu Parekh
GARDEN HISTORY Gordon Campbell
GENES Jonathan Slack
GENIUS Andrew Robinson
GENOMICS John Archibald
GEOFFREY CHAUCER David Wallace
GEOGRAPHY John Matthews and
  David Herbert
GEOLOGY Jan Zalasiewicz
GEOPHYSICS William Lowrie
GEOPOLITICS Klaus Dodds
GERMAN LITERATURE Nicholas Boyle
GERMAN PHILOSOPHY
  Andrew Bowie
GLACIATION David J. A. Evans
GLOBAL CATASTROPHES Bill McGuire
GLOBAL ECONOMIC HISTORY
  Robert C. Allen
GLOBALIZATION Manfred Steger
GOD John Bowker
GOETHE Ritchie Robertson
THE GOTHIC Nick Groom
GOVERNANCE Mark Bevir
GRAVITY Timothy Clifton
THE GREAT DEPRESSION AND THE
  NEW DEAL Eric Rauchway
HABERMAS James Gordon Finlayson
THE HABSBURG EMPIRE
  Martyn Rady
HAPPINESS Daniel M. Haybron
THE HARLEM RENAISSANCE
  Cheryl A. Wall
THE HEBREW BIBLE AS LITERATURE
  Tod Linafelt
HEGEL Peter Singer
HEIDEGGER Michael Inwood

THE HELLENISTIC AGE
Peter Thonemann
HEREDITY John Waller
HERMENEUTICS Jens Zimmermann
HERODOTUS Jennifer T. Roberts
HIEROGLYPHS Penelope Wilson
HINDUISM Kim Knott
HISTORY John H. Arnold
THE HISTORY OF ASTRONOMY
Michael Hoskin
THE HISTORY OF CHEMISTRY
William H. Brock
THE HISTORY OF CHILDHOOD
James Marten
THE HISTORY OF CINEMA
Geoffrey Nowell-Smith
THE HISTORY OF LIFE
Michael Benton
THE HISTORY OF MATHEMATICS
Jacqueline Stedall
THE HISTORY OF MEDICINE
William Bynum
THE HISTORY OF PHYSICS
J. L. Heilbron
THE HISTORY OF TIME
Leofranc Holford-Strevens
HIV AND AIDS Alan Whiteside
HOBBES Richard Tuck
HOLLYWOOD Peter Decherney
THE HOLY ROMAN EMPIRE
Joachim Whaley
HOME Michael Allen Fox
HOMER Barbara Graziosi
HORMONES Martin Luck
HUMAN ANATOMY Leslie Klenerman
HUMAN EVOLUTION Bernard Wood
HUMAN RIGHTS Andrew Clapham
HUMANISM Stephen Law
HUME A. J. Ayer
HUMOUR Noël Carroll
THE ICE AGE Jamie Woodward
IDENTITY Florian Coulmas
IDEOLOGY Michael Freeden
THE IMMUNE SYSTEM
Paul Klenerman
INDIAN CINEMA
Ashish Rajadhyaksha
INDIAN PHILOSOPHY Sue Hamilton
THE INDUSTRIAL REVOLUTION
Robert C. Allen

INFECTIOUS DISEASE Marta L. Wayne
and Benjamin M. Bolker
INFINITY Ian Stewart
INFORMATION Luciano Floridi
INNOVATION Mark Dodgson and
David Gann
INTELLECTUAL PROPERTY
Siva Vaidhyanathan
INTELLIGENCE Ian J. Deary
INTERNATIONAL LAW
Vaughan Lowe
INTERNATIONAL MIGRATION
Khalid Koser
INTERNATIONAL RELATIONS
Paul Wilkinson
INTERNATIONAL SECURITY
Christopher S. Browning
IRAN Ali M. Ansari
ISLAM Malise Ruthven
ISLAMIC HISTORY Adam Silverstein
ISOTOPES Rob Ellam
ITALIAN LITERATURE
Peter Hainsworth and David Robey
JESUS Richard Bauckham
JEWISH HISTORY David N. Myers
JOURNALISM Ian Hargreaves
JUDAISM Norman Solomon
JUNG Anthony Stevens
KABBALAH Joseph Dan
KAFKA Ritchie Robertson
KANT Roger Scruton
KEYNES Robert Skidelsky
KIERKEGAARD Patrick Gardiner
KNOWLEDGE Jennifer Nagel
THE KORAN Michael Cook
KOREA Michael J. Seth
LAKES Warwick F. Vincent
LANDSCAPE ARCHITECTURE
Ian H. Thompson
LANDSCAPES AND
GEOMORPHOLOGY
Andrew Goudie and Heather Viles
LANGUAGES Stephen R. Anderson
LATE ANTIQUITY Gillian Clark
LAW Raymond Wacks
THE LAWS OF THERMODYNAMICS
Peter Atkins
LEADERSHIP Keith Grint
LEARNING Mark Haselgrove
LEIBNIZ Maria Rosa Antognazza

LEO TOLSTOY Liza Knapp
LIBERALISM Michael Freeden
LIGHT Ian Walmsley
LINCOLN Allen C. Guelzo
LINGUISTICS Peter Matthews
LITERARY THEORY Jonathan Culler
LOCKE John Dunn
LOGIC Graham Priest
LOVE Ronald de Sousa
MACHIAVELLI Quentin Skinner
MADNESS Andrew Scull
MAGIC Owen Davies
MAGNA CARTA Nicholas Vincent
MAGNETISM Stephen Blundell
MALTHUS Donald Winch
MAMMALS T. S. Kemp
MANAGEMENT John Hendry
MAO Delia Davin
MARINE BIOLOGY Philip V. Mladenov
THE MARQUIS DE SADE John Phillips
MARTIN LUTHER Scott H. Hendrix
MARTYRDOM Jolyon Mitchell
MARX Peter Singer
MATERIALS Christopher Hall
MATHEMATICAL FINANCE
    Mark H. A. Davis
MATHEMATICS Timothy Gowers
MATTER Geoff Cottrell
THE MEANING OF LIFE
    Terry Eagleton
MEASUREMENT David Hand
MEDICAL ETHICS Michael Dunn and
    Tony Hope
MEDICAL LAW Charles Foster
MEDIEVAL BRITAIN John Gillingham
    and Ralph A. Griffiths
MEDIEVAL LITERATURE
    Elaine Treharne
MEDIEVAL PHILOSOPHY
    John Marenbon
MEMORY Jonathan K. Foster
METAPHYSICS Stephen Mumford
METHODISM William J. Abraham
THE MEXICAN REVOLUTION
    Alan Knight
MICHAEL FARADAY
    Frank A. J. L. James
MICROBIOLOGY Nicholas P. Money
MICROECONOMICS Avinash Dixit
MICROSCOPY Terence Allen

THE MIDDLE AGES Miri Rubin
MILITARY JUSTICE Eugene R. Fidell
MILITARY STRATEGY
    Antulio J. Echevarria II
MINERALS David Vaughan
MIRACLES Yujin Nagasawa
MODERN ARCHITECTURE
    Adam Sharr
MODERN ART David Cottington
MODERN CHINA Rana Mitter
MODERN DRAMA
    Kirsten E. Shepherd-Barr
MODERN FRANCE
    Vanessa R. Schwartz
MODERN INDIA Craig Jeffrey
MODERN IRELAND Senia Pašeta
MODERN ITALY Anna Cento Bull
MODERN JAPAN
    Christopher Goto-Jones
MODERN LATIN AMERICAN
    LITERATURE
    Roberto González Echevarría
MODERN WAR Richard English
MODERNISM Christopher Butler
MOLECULAR BIOLOGY Aysha Divan
    and Janice A. Royds
MOLECULES Philip Ball
MONASTICISM Stephen J. Davis
THE MONGOLS Morris Rossabi
MOONS David A. Rothery
MORMONISM Richard Lyman Bushman
MOUNTAINS Martin F. Price
MUHAMMAD Jonathan A. C. Brown
MULTICULTURALISM Ali Rattansi
MULTILINGUALISM John C. Maher
MUSIC Nicholas Cook
MYTH Robert A. Segal
NAPOLEON David Bell
THE NAPOLEONIC WARS
    Mike Rapport
NATIONALISM Steven Grosby
NATIVE AMERICAN LITERATURE
    Sean Teuton
NAVIGATION Jim Bennett
NAZI GERMANY Jane Caplan
NELSON MANDELA Elleke Boehmer
NEOLIBERALISM Manfred Steger and
    Ravi Roy
NETWORKS Guido Caldarelli and
    Michele Catanzaro

THE NEW TESTAMENT
  Luke Timothy Johnson
THE NEW TESTAMENT AS
  LITERATURE Kyle Keefer
NEWTON Robert Iliffe
NIELS BOHR J. L. Heilbron
NIETZSCHE Michael Tanner
NINETEENTH-CENTURY BRITAIN
  Christopher Harvie and
  H. C. G. Matthew
THE NORMAN CONQUEST
  George Garnett
NORTH AMERICAN INDIANS
  Theda Perdue and Michael D. Green
NORTHERN IRELAND
  Marc Mulholland
NOTHING Frank Close
NUCLEAR PHYSICS Frank Close
NUCLEAR POWER Maxwell Irvine
NUCLEAR WEAPONS
  Joseph M. Siracusa
NUMBERS Peter M. Higgins
NUTRITION David A. Bender
OBJECTIVITY Stephen Gaukroger
OCEANS Dorrik Stow
THE OLD TESTAMENT
  Michael D. Coogan
THE ORCHESTRA D. Kern Holoman
ORGANIC CHEMISTRY
  Graham Patrick
ORGANIZATIONS Mary Jo Hatch
ORGANIZED CRIME
  Georgios A. Antonopoulos and
  Georgios Papanicolaou
ORTHODOX CHRISTIANITY
  A. Edward Siecienski
PAGANISM Owen Davies
PAIN Rob Boddice
THE PALESTINIAN-ISRAELI
  CONFLICT Martin Bunton
PANDEMICS Christian W. McMillen
PARTICLE PHYSICS Frank Close
PAUL E. P. Sanders
PEACE Oliver P. Richmond
PENTECOSTALISM William K. Kay
PERCEPTION Brian Rogers
THE PERIODIC TABLE Eric R. Scerri
PHILOSOPHY Edward Craig
PHILOSOPHY IN THE ISLAMIC
  WORLD Peter Adamson

PHILOSOPHY OF BIOLOGY
  Samir Okasha
PHILOSOPHY OF LAW
  Raymond Wacks
PHILOSOPHY OF SCIENCE
  Samir Okasha
PHILOSOPHY OF RELIGION
  Tim Bayne
PHOTOGRAPHY Steve Edwards
PHYSICAL CHEMISTRY Peter Atkins
PHYSICS Sidney Perkowitz
PILGRIMAGE Ian Reader
PLAGUE Paul Slack
PLANETS David A. Rothery
PLANTS Timothy Walker
PLATE TECTONICS Peter Molnar
PLATO Julia Annas
POETRY Bernard O'Donoghue
POLITICAL PHILOSOPHY
  David Miller
POLITICS Kenneth Minogue
POPULISM Cas Mudde and
  Cristóbal Rovira Kaltwasser
POSTCOLONIALISM Robert Young
POSTMODERNISM Christopher Butler
POSTSTRUCTURALISM
  Catherine Belsey
POVERTY Philip N. Jefferson
PREHISTORY Chris Gosden
PRESOCRATIC PHILOSOPHY
  Catherine Osborne
PRIVACY Raymond Wacks
PROBABILITY John Haigh
PROGRESSIVISM Walter Nugent
PROHIBITION W. J. Rorabaugh
PROJECTS Andrew Davies
PROTESTANTISM Mark A. Noll
PSYCHIATRY Tom Burns
PSYCHOANALYSIS Daniel Pick
PSYCHOLOGY Gillian Butler and
  Freda McManus
PSYCHOLOGY OF MUSIC
  Elizabeth Hellmuth Margulis
PSYCHOPATHY Essi Viding
PSYCHOTHERAPY Tom Burns and
  Eva Burns-Lundgren
PUBLIC ADMINISTRATION
  Stella Z. Theodoulou and Ravi K. Roy
PUBLIC HEALTH Virginia Berridge
PURITANISM Francis J. Bremer

THE QUAKERS Pink Dandelion
QUANTUM THEORY
    John Polkinghorne
RACISM Ali Rattansi
RADIOACTIVITY Claudio Tuniz
RASTAFARI Ennis B. Edmonds
READING Belinda Jack
THE REAGAN REVOLUTION Gil Troy
REALITY Jan Westerhoff
RECONSTRUCTION Allen. C. Guelzo
THE REFORMATION Peter Marshall
RELATIVITY Russell Stannard
RELIGION IN AMERICA Timothy Beal
THE RENAISSANCE Jerry Brotton
RENAISSANCE ART
    Geraldine A. Johnson
RENEWABLE ENERGY Nick Jelley
REPTILES T. S. Kemp
REVOLUTIONS Jack A. Goldstone
RHETORIC Richard Toye
RISK Baruch Fischhoff and John Kadvany
RITUAL Barry Stephenson
RIVERS Nick Middleton
ROBOTICS Alan Winfield
ROCKS Jan Zalasiewicz
ROMAN BRITAIN Peter Salway
THE ROMAN EMPIRE
    Christopher Kelly
THE ROMAN REPUBLIC
    David M. Gwynn
ROMANTICISM Michael Ferber
ROUSSEAU Robert Wokler
RUSSELL A. C. Grayling
RUSSIAN HISTORY Geoffrey Hosking
RUSSIAN LITERATURE
    Catriona Kelly
THE RUSSIAN REVOLUTION
    S. A. Smith
SAINTS Simon Yarrow
SAVANNAS Peter A. Furley
SCEPTICISM Duncan Pritchard
SCHIZOPHRENIA Chris Frith and
    Eve Johnstone
SCHOPENHAUER
    Christopher Janaway
SCIENCE AND RELIGION
    Thomas Dixon
SCIENCE FICTION David Seed
THE SCIENTIFIC REVOLUTION
    Lawrence M. Principe

SCOTLAND Rab Houston
SECULARISM Andrew Copson
SEXUAL SELECTION Marlene Zuk and
    Leigh W. Simmons
SEXUALITY Véronique Mottier
SHAKESPEARE'S COMEDIES
    Bart van Es
SHAKESPEARE'S SONNETS AND
    POEMS Jonathan F. S. Post
SHAKESPEARE'S TRAGEDIES
    Stanley Wells
SIKHISM Eleanor Nesbitt
THE SILK ROAD James A. Millward
SLANG Jonathon Green
SLEEP Steven W. Lockley and
    Russell G. Foster
SOCIAL AND CULTURAL
    ANTHROPOLOGY
    John Monaghan and Peter Just
SOCIAL PSYCHOLOGY Richard J. Crisp
SOCIAL WORK Sally Holland and
    Jonathan Scourfield
SOCIALISM Michael Newman
SOCIOLINGUISTICS John Edwards
SOCIOLOGY Steve Bruce
SOCRATES C. C. W. Taylor
SOUND Mike Goldsmith
SOUTHEAST ASIA James R. Rush
THE SOVIET UNION Stephen Lovell
THE SPANISH CIVIL WAR
    Helen Graham
SPANISH LITERATURE Jo Labanyi
SPINOZA Roger Scruton
SPIRITUALITY Philip Sheldrake
SPORT Mike Cronin
STARS Andrew King
STATISTICS David J. Hand
STEM CELLS Jonathan Slack
STOICISM Brad Inwood
STRUCTURAL ENGINEERING
    David Blockley
STUART BRITAIN John Morrill
SUPERCONDUCTIVITY
    Stephen Blundell
SUPERSTITION Stuart Vyse
SYMMETRY Ian Stewart
SYNAESTHESIA Julia Simner
SYNTHETIC BIOLOGY Jamie A. Davies
TAXATION Stephen Smith
TEETH Peter S. Ungar

TELESCOPES Geoff Cottrell
TERRORISM Charles Townshend
THEATRE Marvin Carlson
THEOLOGY David F. Ford
THINKING AND REASONING
  Jonathan St B. T. Evans
THOMAS AQUINAS Fergus Kerr
THOUGHT Tim Bayne
TIBETAN BUDDHISM
  Matthew T. Kapstein
TIDES David George Bowers and
  Emyr Martyn Roberts
TOCQUEVILLE Harvey C. Mansfield
TOPOLOGY Richard Earl
TRAGEDY Adrian Poole
TRANSLATION Matthew Reynolds
THE TREATY OF VERSAILLES
  Michael S. Neiberg
TRIGONOMETRY
  Glen Van Brummelen
THE TROJAN WAR Eric H. Cline
TRUST Katherine Hawley
THE TUDORS John Guy
TWENTIETH-CENTURY BRITAIN
  Kenneth O. Morgan
TYPOGRAPHY Paul Luna
THE UNITED NATIONS
  Jussi M. Hanhimäki
UNIVERSITIES AND COLLEGES
  David Palfreyman and Paul Temple
THE U.S. CONGRESS Donald A. Ritchie

THE U.S. CONSTITUTION
  David J. Bodenhamer
THE U.S. SUPREME COURT
  Linda Greenhouse
UTILITARIANISM
  Katarzyna de Lazari-Radek and
  Peter Singer
UTOPIANISM Lyman Tower Sargent
VETERINARY SCIENCE
  James Yeates
THE VIKINGS Julian D. Richards
VIRUSES Dorothy H. Crawford
VOLTAIRE Nicholas Cronk
WAR AND TECHNOLOGY
  Alex Roland
WATER John Finney
WAVES Mike Goldsmith
WEATHER Storm Dunlop
THE WELFARE STATE David Garland
WILLIAM SHAKESPEARE
  Stanley Wells
WITCHCRAFT Malcolm Gaskill
WITTGENSTEIN A. C. Grayling
WORK Stephen Fineman
WORLD MUSIC Philip Bohlman
THE WORLD TRADE
  ORGANIZATION Amrita Narlikar
WORLD WAR II Gerhard L. Weinberg
WRITING AND SCRIPT
  Andrew Robinson
ZIONISM Michael Stanislawski

Available soon:

SMELL Matthew Cobb
THE SUN Philip Judge
DEMENTIA Kathleen Taylor

NUMBER THEORY
  Robin Wilson
FIRE Andrew C. Scott

For more information visit our website

www.oup.com/vsi/

Jim Fraser

FORENSIC SCIENCE

A Very Short Introduction

SECOND EDITION

OXFORD
UNIVERSITY PRESS

OXFORD
UNIVERSITY PRESS

Great Clarendon Street, Oxford, OX2 6DP,
United Kingdom

Oxford University Press is a department of the University of Oxford.
It furthers the University's objective of excellence in research, scholarship,
and education by publishing worldwide. Oxford is a registered trade mark of
Oxford University Press in the UK and in certain other countries

Published in the United States of America by Oxford University Press
198 Madison Avenue, New York, NY 10016, United States of America

British Library Cataloguing in Publication Data
Data available

Library of Congress Control Number: 2019955396

ISBN 978-0-19-883441-0

Printed in Great Britain by
Ashford Colour Press Ltd, Gosport, Hampshire

Links to third party websites are provided by Oxford in good faith and
for information only. Oxford disclaims any responsibility for the materials
contained in any third party website referenced in this work.

For my family

Contents

Preface and acknowledgements to second edition xvii

Preface and acknowledgements to first edition xix

List of illustrations xxiii

1 What is forensic science? 1

2 Investigating crime 8

3 Crime scene management and forensic investigation 17

4 Laboratory examination: search, recovery, analysis 31

5 DNA profiling and databases 46

6 Prints and marks: more ways to identify people and things 65

7 Trace evidence 81

8 Drugs and toxicology 93

9 Science and justice—a case study 107

References 113

Further reading 115

Index 117

Preface and acknowledgements to second edition

Much seems to have changed since the first edition of this book a decade ago. DNA technology has continued to develop and is now more sensitive and discriminating than ever before. Digital forensics has become embedded in police investigations and continues to grow without apparent limits. Legislation such as the Psychoactive Substances Act 2016 now requires the analysis and identification of many new illicit substances. There have also been developments that were less positive. The National Academies of Sciences (NAS) reviewed forensic science in the USA and raised many concerns about practices, standards, and knowledge in that country. Their report described a fragmented and inexplicably variable sector with arcane and unjustifiable practices. Many of these issues arose from the distinctive characteristics of the legal systems in the USA but there were also many general findings of relevance to other jurisdictions. Over the decade since the report was published, research has continued to confirm many of its findings. We can add to the NAS report findings, particular difficulties encountered with fingerprint examinations in the McKie and Mayfield cases in Scotland and the USA. All of these issues continue to shape how forensic science is used in investigations, in the laboratory, and in court.

In the first edition I tried to balance some of the more optimistic presentations of forensic science that the general reader might encounter in both fact and fiction with a more nuanced perspective. I continue this theme in the second edition. The assumption that all forensic science (whatever that may be) is always objective, reliable, and useful is in my view both over simplistic and over optimistic.

The text has been extensively revised. I have added new material; two new chapters, drugs and toxicology (Chapter 8) and a case study (Chapter 9). To make space for this new material I have simplified the text elsewhere without, I hope, diminishing its content. I have reduced the number of tables and simplified some that are retained. Finally, I have introduced numerous case examples, mostly from my personal experience, which show the real life use of forensic evidence.

I am grateful for the help and advice of many individuals including Steven Ferguson, Penny Haddrill, Judy Livingstone, Chris Mills, Jane Officer, Angela Shaw, Denise Syndercombe-Court, Bill Tilstone, Hazel Torrance, Craig Wilson, and Robin Williams. I also want to thank Latha Menon and Jenny Nugee at OUP for their continued support.

Preface and acknowledgements to first edition

There is more interest in forensic science now than at any previous time in its history. There are more students studying 'forensic' courses in the UK than ever before and there is a seemingly endless list of TV dramas that are testimony to huge popular interest in the subject. In real life, forensic science attracts enormous media attention in high-profile cases such as the deaths of Jill Dando (Chapter 9), and Rachel Nickell (Chapters 4 and 7). More importantly, forensic science provides 'leads' in police investigations and evidence for prosecutions that were previously unimaginable. Despite this, understanding of forensic science is poor even amongst those, such as lawyers and police officers, who are required to use it, as well as others such as politicians and journalists. Public understanding of the subject is largely based on TV shows, such as *CSI* (*Crime Scene Investigation*), which use hi-tech imagery for dramatic effect at the expense of understanding an increasingly important part of the criminal justice process. There is even the so-called 'CSI effect'—that expectations and misconceptions about forensic science on the part of the public may have adverse influence on jury decisions.

Dramatic scientific breakthroughs, particularly the discovery of DNA profiling, in the past twenty years or so have revolutionized forensic science. Evidence can be obtained from microscopic traces of body fluids, drugs, and explosives of sufficient quality for it to be pivotal in an investigation or trial. There has been a parallel revolution in how the police investigate crime. It is probably more effective, faster, and more reliable to investigate the crimes that affect us most (burglary, car theft, and suchlike) using DNA and fingerprints than by any other means. In major crime, such as homicide, forensic scientists have moved from being backroom boffins to the forefront of international investigations. Forensic science is now firmly embedded in the criminal justice agenda since it can answer investigative questions in many instances better than any other means available. It is a complex activity at the interface of science and law. Forensic science is not a discipline in its own right, but engages many disciplines such as chemistry, molecular biology, and engineering, though it has a number of distinctive features. Whilst rooted in science, it is an intensely practical activity that deals with real-world issues: explosions, blood spatters, bodies, and stolen cars. Complex scientific findings must be weighed carefully and dispassionately, and communicated with clarity, simplicity, and precision to police, lawyers, jurors, and the judiciary. Forensic science encounters all aspects of human behaviour. The apocryphal headline 'all human life is here' fits forensic science very well: the plain stupid (the killers who panicked and reburied a body for the third time in a flower bed in a graveyard); the unlucky (the man who wrote an anonymous threatening letter to the chairman of a London football club on paper with invisible indented impressions of his name and home address); to the cold and frighteningly malevolent—serial sexual offenders and killers who plan and fantasize about their crime throughout the course of their life, such as Robert Black (Chapter 7). In short, forensic science matters because the link to everyday life (and death) is more direct, tangible, and visible. But forensic science does not have all the answers. In some instances, it has no answers at all (for example in the Michael Stone case; Chapters 1 and 3), and in some cases it fails spectacularly and worryingly for reasons that are not always clear, for example in the Jill Dando case. Forensic science is also regarded ambivalently by some (as is science by the public in general) and by others as a source of injustice. The arguments of the latter are rarely well informed in my experience, but I will explore some of these issues in this book.

It would be impossible to do justice to all areas of forensic science in a book of this type and length, so I have necessarily had to select some things and exclude others. Whole areas of forensic science are completely absent: toxicology, crash investigation, computer forensics, document examination, and others are dealt with superficially or in passing. In making this selection, I have attempted to identify the central issues of forensic science, such as identification and evidence evaluation, and its main procedures and mechanisms, such as continuity of evidence (chain of custody in the USA and many other countries) and minimizing contamination. Many of the cases I have used as illustrations come from direct personal involvement and memory. I have not provided detailed information in every case as this is rarely necessary to gain an understanding, but in some instances the full details are already well publicized. It is my contention that you do not need to know the details of every area of forensic science to know the nature of forensic science. I will leave the reader to judge the success or otherwise of my efforts.

Although science uses more or less universal terminology, that used in policing and the law varies considerably even to the extent that the same word can mean different things in different jurisdictions. For example, the document containing forensic science evidence presented to the courts in England is called a 'statement', whereas the equivalent document in Scots Law is called a 'joint report' and a statement means something else. In Scotland, items produced in evidence are called 'productions', whereas in England, the USA, Australia, and many other countries they are called 'exhibits'. This is a constant problem when discussing or teaching forensic science. To overcome this, I have decided to abandon all attempts to be legally precise except where essential and have used common-sense terminology such as item (instead of production or exhibit) or report (instead of 'joint report' or 'statement'). None of these infringements should impede understanding of the subject. The chapters generally follow the chronological flow of how forensic science interacts with the criminal law—incident, investigation, and laboratory analysis—from crime scene to court.

Finally, a word on those 'CSI' or 'eureka' moments—when the scientist 'cracks' the case with a piece of brilliant incisiveness and basks in the admiration of their colleagues. Yes, they happen, but far less frequently than TV dramas would have you believe. Perhaps five or six times in a long career this might occur. In truth, most cases are solved by a combination of systematic investigation by a range of professionals (police officers, scientists, pathologists, CSIs), good teamwork, effective leadership, hard work, and some luck. I hope this comes across from the text.

I am indebted to many for their support in the writing of this book: the initial reviewers, colleagues, friends, and all who provided advice, critical comment, and images. I wish to thank them all (in alphabetical order): Sarah Cresswell, Peter Gill, Jim Govan, Isobel Hamilton, Max Houck, Anya Hunt, Lester Knibb, Adrian Linacre, Terry Napier, Niamh NicDaeid, James Robertson, Derek Scrimger, Nigel Watson, Robin Williams. I would also like to thank Latha Menon for her enthusiasm in commissioning the project and Emma Marchant for seeing it through with me.

List of illustrations

1 Loss of fibres from the surface of the skin **3**
Courtesy of the Chartered Society of Forensic Sciences.

2 Shoe mark in sand **15**

3 Shoe mark in wet concrete **16**

4. Triangulation of bloodstains **28**

5 Sperm and vaginal cells stained with haematoxylin and eosin **40**

6 Physical fit of two parts of a petrol receipt **44**

7 The structure of DNA, its relationship with chromosomes, and location within the cell **48**

8 The polymerase chain reaction **51**
© MedPrepOnline.com

9 DNA kinship analysis **55**

10 DNA mixed stain analysis **56**

11 Striations on bullet casing **66**
US Department of Justice.

12 Fingerprint ridge patterns **71**
Scottish Police Services Authority Forensic Services.

13 Fingerprint minutiae **72**
Scottish Police Services Authority Forensic Services.

14 Comparison microscope **85**
Courtesy of Leica Microsystems.

15 Colour spectra of blue acrylic fibres using microspectrophotometry **86**
Courtesy of the Chartered Society of Forensic Sciences.

16 Relative risk of fatal car crash by age and blood alcohol level **100**
Source: Ministry of Transport, New Zealand, Alcohol/Drugs crash statistics for the year ended 31 December 2010.

Chapter 1
What is forensic science?

Klaus Mann (the son of Thomas Mann) discovered the corpse of his former lover who had shot himself through the heart. He recalled that 'The bloodstains looked like the scattered fragments of a mysterious pattern—a last message, a warning, the writing on the wall'. Many believe the role of forensic science is to interpret such patterns, to read their 'message'. Edmond Locard (1877–1976) was one of the most influential thinkers in forensic science. Locard established the first police scientific laboratory for investigating crime scenes in Lyon, France, in 1910. He also set out what many consider to be the fundamental basis and guiding principle of forensic science. This is most frequently formulated as 'every contact leaves a trace', although Locard never used these exact words.

Paul Kirk, an American forensic scientist, expressed similar sentiments to Locard and Mann in even more detail and in more utilitarian terms:

> Wherever he steps, whatever he touches, whatever he leaves, even unconsciously, will serve as a silent witness against him. Not only his fingerprints or his footprints, but his hair, the fibres from his clothes, the glass he breaks, the tool mark he leaves, the paint he scratches, the blood or semen he deposits or collects. All of these and more, bear mute witness against him. This is evidence that

does not forget. It is not confused by the excitement of the moment. It is not absent because human witnesses are. It is factual evidence. Physical evidence cannot be wrong, it cannot perjure itself, it cannot be wholly absent. Only human failure to find it, study and understand it, can diminish its value.

This is one of the most commonly used (and misattributed) quotes in forensic science. Not only is there a story to be told but, according to Kirk, one cannot fail to read it. Directly or by implication, the message that is commonly taught to police officers and forensic science students is that these views represent reality: that there will always be evidence about such events, and ultimately that all things can be known about a crime or a criminal. Only failure on our part as humans can usurp this aim. Furthermore this evidence is dispassionate, objective: not only will we know things, there will only be one version of the truth (and therefore no disputes). And we have the last laugh since all this can happen without the criminal even knowing.

Do you believe this? Is it possible? My colleague Robin Williams calls this the 'forensic imaginary'—the conviction that all events can be reconstructed from forensic evidence, that there is always a decipherable last message from the victim and evidence from the perpetrator; the 'signature' of the killer.

From my experience of forensic science, it is difficult to imagine a situation that is much further from reality. Locard's principle as it is usually described is not a scientific theory because it cannot be tested by scientific means, and it cannot predict in the way that scientific laws such as gravity or electromagnetism can. Nor could it be described as a model of the world—we would need much more evidence than we actually have to assert this. It is more a principle based on a thought experiment. Like other 'scientific' principles, for example the cosmological principle, which makes certain simplifying (but untrue) assumptions about the distribution of matter in the universe, the point of it is to help us think about things when we have little or no data to go on. What we do know is that research supports Locard's assertions in part but that there are also limitations to the application of these concepts. The flawed assumption is that once evidence is transferred it remains in place, because we know that this is not the case. Generally speaking, such evidence will be lost and often very quickly, perhaps a few hours after the event, as illustrated in Figure 1. We can therefore put forward as a genuine scientific theory, one that can be tested on the basis of empirical evidence, the concept of transfer and persistence. For example, when items of clothing come into contact, fibres will be transferred from each to the other and then gradually lost.

We have perhaps been a little hard on Locard and Kirk. So let's return to this with a thought experiment and imagine a world in which things are constantly being transferred, and as we now know also lost.

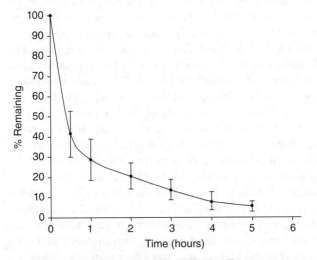

1. Loss of fibres from the surface of the skin. This illustrates a pattern which is typical of fibre loss from many different surfaces. After five hours around 95 per cent of the evidence has been lost.

I sit on a fabric-covered seat on a train reading a book. Fibres from my clothing are transferred to the seat and from the seat to my clothing. When I arrive in my office, some fibres which remain on my clothing from the train seat will be transferred to my office seat. So far so good, this is not too complicated, so let's continue with the experiment. Also being transferred to the train seat were fibres from my home environment, from upholstery, carpets, the clothing of my family, and maybe hairs from pets. And on the train seat, as well as fibres from passengers will be fibres from *their* homes, some of which will transfer to my clothing and maybe to my office seat. Now it's quite complicated. There are fibres in my office from people on the train whom I have never been in contact with and who have never been in my office (although most of the fibres will be lost on the walk from the station). There may be fibres from things in my home in other people's offices (who were also on the train). All of these fibres will be mass produced so none of them is unique. It should be clear now that finding fibres that match someone's clothing in my office does not mean that that person has been in my office. In fact, it does not even mean that they have come from that person's clothing. To make sense of any fibres that are found, we need to bring in some modern concepts in forensic work: primary (direct) and secondary (indirect) transfer. The fibres transferred from my clothing to the train seat (and the reverse) are due to direct transfer. The fibres from other people's clothing on my office seat are from indirect transfer. So whilst every (direct) contact may leave a trace, traces may also be transferred which are not due to (direct) contact. The same principles apply to DNA (deoxyribonucleic acid) traces. Finding a DNA profile that matches me on a gun does not mean that I must have handled the gun. The DNA may have been transferred indirectly from another item. Deciding whether traces are from direct or indirect contact requires more information and we will explore this later. Making sense of all this involves uncertain information, scientific tests with inherent uncertainty, and subjective interpretation of test results made by fallible humans. The final twist to this tale is that all of these activities, examinations, and interpretations must comply with the law and legal procedure.

This takes science from the laboratory into a very different world in which the interpretation of the scientific evidence may depend on the law. For although science is essentially universal—it is the same in Glasgow, New York, and Beijing—the law is local and surprisingly variable (at least to scientists). Furthermore in common law systems such as those in the UK, USA, Australia, and Canada, the rules of evidence constrain what can be said in court, including what scientific or expert evidence can be presented. The law decides for itself what can and cannot be heard. And fundamental to the common law is the adversarial process and the notion that argument is the best way to get to the bottom of what any set of facts means. The law is the final nail in the coffin for Kirk and Locard and any grand vision of certainty, objectivity, and infallibility. But we should acknowledge their originality, creative imagination, insight, and the influence they have had in inspiring scientists to develop more rigorous empirically based theories.

Much of forensic science is aimed at identifying things—people, objects, substances—but what do we mean by 'identify'? Identity means different things to different people and has a common-sense usage (which varies depending on context) as well as philosophical interpretations. Identity is central to the criminal justice process since we must be certain that a person arrested or found guilty is unequivocally who we believe them to be (irrespective of who they say they are). So what do the terms 'identity' or 'identify' mean to a forensic scientist? You may be surprised to find that it depends whom you ask, and that different disciplines within forensic science use different standards and criteria to identify things. Although the terms are not universally used, most forensic scientists will draw a distinction between classification of things (placing an object in a defined category) and identification (the recognition of uniqueness—that something is *one* of a kind).

Classification can be a continuous process—a car, a red car, a red sports car, a red sports car with damaged bodywork—which increasingly moves towards narrower or smaller categories; whereas identification is a final and categoric determination of uniqueness—*the* red sports car with the damaged bodywork abandoned at the scene of the crash. There is only one such vehicle.

Some forensic scientists, especially in the USA, use another word which helps avoid some of this confusion—'individualization'. This was coined by Paul Kirk and has the benefit of being unambiguous. If you individualize something, it is one of a kind, unique; it has not merely been classified, no matter how few things there are in the class. Kirk suggested that individualization is the primary aim of forensic science, but this cannot be the full story. There are very many instances when individualization cannot take place for reasons of practicality or technological limitations, and there are many instances when individualization is not necessary to answer an investigative question. Many experienced forensic scientists consider that answering investigative questions is the aim of forensic science, irrespective of how this is done, and this is a view I share. Evidence that falls a long way short of individualization can be relevant and valuable in a criminal inquiry. In the Michael Stone case (Chapter 3) it was known that the killer had searched through the family's belongings including the children's lunch boxes. A partial fingermark in blood was found inside one of the lunchboxes. The fingermark contained too little information to identify anyone but had sufficient detail to eliminate Stone, an important fact for the defence case.

So what is forensic science? Definitions don't usually help because they often evoke a connection between law and science without providing much insight into the complexities of this odd relationship. I think it is better to describe than define. For me, forensic science is the investigation, explanation, and evaluation of events of legal relevance including the identity, origin, life history, and interactions of humans, materials (e.g. paint, plastics), substances (e.g. drugs and poisons), and artefacts (e.g. clothing, shoes). This is done using a variety of techniques or methodologies, *some* of which are scientific, which allow us to describe, infer, and reconstruct events. The reconstruction is based on the analysis and evaluation of indirect fragmentary physical evidence (what remains of the traces) and relevant information. From these facts, established to some pre-determined legal standard, the law infers behaviour, motivation, and criminal intent. In short, forensic science answers the central questions in a criminal investigation: who, what, where, when, why, and how? Answers to these questions include the identity of the criminal or victim using DNA profiling or fingerprints, what type of shoe left the mark at the crime scene, the sequence of events that led to a death as established by bloodstain pattern analysis, where a shot was fired from, or how a fire has started, and why it burned so fiercely, from analysis of flammable liquids. We will consider many of these issues in more detail in subsequent chapters, describing the processes involved, the methods of analysis, how the evidence is interpreted, and ultimately how it is presented in court.

Chapter 2
Investigating crime

Forensic science takes place within the complexities and procedures of the law, its timescales, pressures, and contingencies, the drama of a criminal investigation, and occasionally in the intense glare of the media. This chapter explains how the police investigate crime, setting out some of the principles and procedures involved and how forensic science provides answers to the important questions we identified at the end of Chapter 1. Science is the best means we have of describing and understanding the physical world, and forensic science has fundamentally changed the way the police investigate crime, legally, procedurally, and conceptually, because it can answer many of these important questions faster and more objectively than by any other means.

A crime is a breach of the criminal law that requires two elements: a mental element (*mens rea*—a guilty mind) and a physical element (*actus reus*—the guilty act). It's not possible to directly establish *mens rea* using physical science—this must be inferred from the activities and behaviour of the accused. To commit a crime, the accused must have the intent to do wrong and to carry out the act. A criminal investigation is a search for information with the aim of bringing an offender to justice, which is achieved by reconstructing the events leading up to, during, and sometimes after the crime. This is done by gathering facts and information, speaking to witnesses, extracting data from CCTV and phones, recovering documents, and carrying out scientific examinations, with the aim of answering the most important questions: who? what? why? when? where? how? Effective investigations require skills, resources, and time. Complex investigations such as serial offences and homicides also need coordination and planning during both the investigation and the trial. Most serious crimes will be investigated by a team of detectives and specialist police officers led by a senior investigating officer (SIO)—an experienced and trained detective.

In the UK and many other countries, the police have systems and procedures in place to help achieve their aims. The modern approach to investigating major crime in the UK followed serious problems in the investigation of the 'Yorkshire Ripper' case in the 1980s. In pre-computer days, the police were overwhelmed by paper records and unable to link together important findings from thousands of separate 'leads' or to track the outcomes of various aspects of the investigation. This (as well as a number of investigative failings) delayed the arrest and prosecution of Peter Sutcliffe, who was subsequently convicted. A review carried out following the trial recommended major changes in procedure that included the use of standard operating procedures in major inquiries, introduction of computer systems (HOLMES—Home Office Large Major Enquiry System), and a new specialist scientific role in complex inquiries to ensure that forensic science is focused on the primary objectives of the investigation.

Forensic science also came to public prominence following high-profile miscarriages of justice in England in the 1990s. One of these cases, the 'Birmingham Six', who were wrongly convicted of terrorist offences, included specific failings in the scientific aspects of the investigation. Following a Royal Commission which considered this case and others, there were radical changes in English law and forensic science practices. The main change with respect to forensic science was the introduction of formal quality assurance systems to standardize laboratory practices. In legal terms, the Police and Criminal Evidence Act (1984) was introduced to specify how the police deal with accused persons, go about their investigations, and are accountable for their actions. These and other changes have led the police to take an approach which is based on the systematic elimination of individuals from an investigation (trace, interview, eliminate—TIE) until one person is left who may be the offender. If we take a homicide as an example, there will be a number of individuals who will be high on the list for TIE, such as:

- those who had access to the scene at the time of the crime;
- known associates of the victim or those living locally;
- individuals with previous convictions, especially for violence;
- those with physical characteristics similar to the suspected offender;
- owners of vehicles of the same type as that known or suspected to be involved.

The TIE process, when applied systematically, gradually accumulates vast amounts of information of increasingly fine granularity on the identity, behaviour, activities, relationships, and history of individuals. This includes information such as where they work, who they go drinking with, what their hobbies are, who they are having affairs with, who is in debt, who has suddenly come into money, who has recently had a dispute or fight. Such inquiries will also reveal relationships between people, and places and objects of interest to the inquiry such as vehicles or crime scenes. Much of this information is of no interest to the police as they will be focused on what is required to be established to detect and then prosecute the particular offence. TIE actions are combined with other common investigative lines such as house-to-house inquiries (canvassing) and tracing local individuals with convictions for similar offences (*modus operandi* suspects).

All relevant lines of inquiry are identified and logged on the computer specially developed for this purpose—HOLMES. This is then used to aid prioritizing of the most important inquiries, the allocation of tasks to specific officers, and the recording of the outcomes from these tasks. All information is then stored in a single database which can be interrogated and used to develop and test hypotheses. HOLMES also helps identify facts and witnesses which corroborate each other, as well as inconsistencies, for example in witness accounts, which can then be re-investigated.

The information that comes from these inquiries can be fragmentary and incomplete; not all things are knowable. The analogy of investigation most frequently used is that of a jigsaw puzzle—so long as you have the pieces, only time and persistence are required to solve the puzzle. This is a poor analogy for such a complex event as a major crime for a number of reasons. Even when the crime is solved and prosecuted, the puzzle is rarely complete. In the Michael Stone case (Chapter 3) the weapon was never found. The body of Suzanne Pilley (see below) has never been found. Nor does the puzzle need to be complete, since the law does not expect the answer to every question but proof of the key facts and elimination of reasonable alternatives. And these facts will be rendered in an adversarial legal process in which there are always two sides to any story: there is always an alternative explanation, always some missing piece of the problem. Investigations and trials are contingent, restricted by the rules of evidence and procedure, and limited by time and resources. A trial is only a search for the truth in this narrow sense.

Investigation of many different types of crime can be supported or resolved by a wide range of forensic analyses that can provide the answers to who, what, why, when, where, and how?

On 4 May 2010, 38-year-old Suzanne Pilley made her way from her home in Edinburgh to her workplace in the city. CCTV showed Suzanne's route to within 20 metres of her office but she never arrived at her desk. She was reported missing that evening. Following her disappearance there was no activity on her phone nor were her bank or credit cards used. On 23 May her work colleague and former partner David Gilroy was arrested. Their relationship had been stormy and Pilley had tried to end it. Gilroy had scratches on his face. Phone records showed that Gilroy was in constant contact with Pilley, sometimes texting her more than fifty times a day. This contact stopped the day before Pilley went missing. Gilroy went several times to the office basement on 4 May and then left unexpectedly in his car to travel to Lochgilphead on the west coast of Scotland, around 130 miles from Edinburgh. He said this was a business trip but no one else in his office was aware of these plans. Investigators used CCTV to reconstruct the car journey. They also established that the journey took two hours longer than it ought to have taken and used more fuel than would have been needed. Gilroy did not explain why he made the journey nor why it took so long. No DNA matching Pilley was found in Gilroy's car but the forensic scientist noticed that the boot had a fresh smell that could have been from a cleaning agent. The jury deliberated for two and a half days before finding Gilroy guilty of the murder. Suzanne Pilley's body has never been found and is believed to have been hidden somewhere on the route to Lochgilphead. This case illustrates some of the different types of evidence that investigators use to reconstruct a case and the increasing importance of digital evidence.

Mobile phones and CCTV are among the first types of evidence that investigators look for. When a phone is switched on it logs on to its provider network via the nearest base station antenna or 'cell site'. Cell sites store metadata from any call made. This metadata includes: type of call (text message, email, internet access, download), call details (date, time, length), outgoing and receiving numbers, mobile device identity (IMEI number), and cell site identity.

All of this can be used to determine the location of a phone, when it is being used, and who or what it is connecting with. This information can be used to connect individuals (calls, texts, emails), reveal internet browsing habits, link an individual to a location, or track the movements of an individual. Cell site analysis cannot always pinpoint the exact location of a phone directly but by using data from multiple cell sites this can be inferred, sometimes very accurately. If a phone is retrieved it may be possible to recover data from it such as text messages, email, images. The likelihood of accessing such data depends on a variety of factors including the type and condition of the phone and whether the original data has been deleted or is encrypted.

The UK has more CCTV cameras per head of population than any other country in the world. CCTV is located in public and private locations including homes, offices, shops, railway stations, buses, trains, airports, ferry terminals, and countless other places. CCTV is routinely used in the investigation of many crimes to locate, identify, and track victims and perpetrators. Occasionally, CCTV also captures the crime in action.

Another area of evidence that is of growing importance is the analysis of social media. Facebook, Instagram, Twitter, WhatsApp, and many other apps can now provide a record of communication and interactions between individuals that may be part of or leading up to a crime. They can help establish if someone who has gone missing is still alive, and they can provide evidence of the planning of crimes such as grooming.

The technologies described above are most commonly referred to collectively as digital forensics. Digital forensics involves the extraction and interpretation of data from a constantly growing and changing list of devices such as tablets, SATNAV, fitbits, smart watches, desktop computers, and computer networks. Police knew what time David Gilroy arrived in work because he logged in to his network computer. Digital analysis can also reveal how we interact with computer systems and databases in everyday activities such as purchasing goods and services (credit card, debit card, contactless card, phone pay) and how we are identified for various purposes (passports, workplace access, club membership).

Although digital forensics has opened up new and productive ways of investigating crime it comes with a number of inherent problems. The list of different devices from which digital data can be extracted is long, growing, and rapidly evolving. As well as the devices mentioned above this includes hard drives, solid state drives, USB drives, CD, DVD, and any other storage media. The method of data extraction depends on the type of device and often requires specialist knowledge and software. The volume of data that devices in everyday use can store presents an ongoing problem for the investigator. A typical smartphone can store thousands of emails, text messages, and images; it is often completely impractical to fully examine a device. Finally, encryption of data can render analysis all but impossible. Storage media are easily encrypted as are some apps such as WhatsApp. Cloud storage servers such as Dropbox are also often encrypted which means that any data can only be recovered from the original device. In the digital domain we also leave a trail that investigators can follow and reconstruct. I have given only a limited indication of the potential of digital forensics, which is now the largest and most rapidly expanding area of forensic practice.

Most cases will be solved by combinations of evidence, for example linking an individual to a mobile phone using DNA or fingerprints and cell site analysis to show where the individual was when the phone was being used. Some cases require comparatively straightforward questions to be answered: could the shoes seized by the police have made the marks at the crime scene? Others ask much more complex questions: what was the sequence of events leading to a death? The detailed context of the case will determine which questions will be asked by the police and therefore which scientific tests will have to be carried out.

The case context will also determine the true value of the forensic evidence to an investigation. The specific details of the incident—timings, locations, other evidence—and alternative explanations must all be considered to form the final evaluation of the significance of the evidence.

This idea of context is more easily explained by images than in words, as can be seen in Figures 2 and 3. Both images show marks which can be used to identify the type of shoe that made them and potentially link the mark to the actual shoe. The deposition of both marks can also be timed accurately or at least within certain limits. One is in sand on a beach and could only have been made between tides. The other is in concrete (on a wall at the same beach) and could only have been made when this was wet. One mark is transient and will persist only for a few hours, the other is a permanent feature of the location. It is not the shoe mark in isolation that determines the significance of the evidence, but the mark together with the surrounding context.

2. Shoe mark in sand.

3. Shoe mark in wet concrete.

In Chapter 3, beginning at the crime scene, we will explore how the police investigation and the scientific analyses are integrated to address the main issues in a case.

Chapter 3
Crime scene management and forensic investigation

Forensic science is driven by questions that arise outside the scientific laboratory in messy, distracting, and difficult situations such as crime scenes. To maximize potential evidence in an investigation, the process must begin at the crime scene. The purpose of crime scene management is to control, preserve, record, and recover evidence and intelligence from the scene of an incident in accordance with the law, and to appropriate professional and ethical standards. Although generally called 'crime scene management', strictly speaking we should refer to this as 'incident scene management', as some scenes, such as an accidental gas explosion, are not crimes. In other instances, the central question of the investigation may be: is this a crime?—so pre-judging the issue is unwise. For simplicity, we will refer to any scene as a crime scene whilst acknowledging that this is loose terminology.

In their physical characteristics, scenes are hugely varied, but typical ones include houses, cars, and commercial premises. Less common examples of real scenes I have investigated are fields, secure mental health institutions, railway carriages, and motorways. Each type of scene presents different demands in how it is managed, but the most significant issue is why the scene is being examined. In many investigations there is more than one scene. In a homicide, as well as where the body is found, the suspect's home and vehicle are potential crime scenes.

The person ultimately responsible for the scene is the investigating officer, who is invariably a police officer. In serious and major crime in the UK, the SIO works closely with a number of specialists, particularly the crime scene manager (CSM), who is responsible for advising on the detailed approach to the scene. This includes the investigative potential of different types of forensic evidence, the value of experts in particular fields such as ballistics, blood patterns, or fire investigation, and the coordination of all aspects of the scene examination. It entails arranging and managing the post-mortem examination, agreeing the forensic strategy with the SIO, and maintaining ongoing communication with forensic science laboratories, individual experts, and the investigation team. Crime scene management in major crimes is physically and mentally demanding and requires high levels of knowledge of investigation and forensic science, excellent planning skills, good interpersonal communication, and team leadership. A CSM at a major incident will have a team of crime scene investigators (CSIs) to carry out the necessary examinations.

Subject to the scene being safe to enter, the first stage of crime scene management is to secure the scene and ensure that it is preserved in the condition that is closest to the original state when the crime took place. This means clearing away any witnesses and bystanders who are present and making sure that no one else enters who does not have legitimate reason to do so. Physical security of the scene is managed by two sets of cordons. These are around the immediate (inner) scene (such as the house where a body has been found) and an area that is deemed relevant to the investigation and which may be much wider. This might include a street or part of a field. This outer cordon acts as a general control point in the early stages of the incident to ensure access is limited. A log is maintained, usually by a police officer at the inner scene, of all who enter, at what time, and for what purpose. This is a formal legal document, and will be produced and may be inspected in any subsequent trial. Crime scenes attract a great deal of interest from those who have no right to be there, including busybodies, the media, and sometimes the offender. These basic security precautions control access, maintain the integrity of the scene, and minimize disturbance, interference, and contamination.

The scene must be accurately recorded in as near a state to the original as possible before the examination starts. There is a legal requirement (or at least an expectation) that a detailed record of the scene is available to the prosecution and the defence in any trial. The records are also used to brief those involved in the investigation who were unable to enter the crime scene. The records are also essential for the reconstruction and interpretation of the incident. The scene is recorded using documents (notes, plans, diagrams, witness statements), images (stills, video, and other specialist means), and sometimes audio notes also. All of these records serve to establish a contemporaneous record of the incident at the time of discovery and initial investigation.

Recovery of the evidence then begins in a planned sequence using an agreed search strategy. Since there are likely to be several people involved, it is essential that they each understand their particular role and that the entire scene is covered completely and systematically. What is recovered (and what is being searched for) will be related to the nature of the incident. Some of these things will be obvious—in a homicide by stabbing, finding the weapon will be high on the priority list, as would be bullets in a shooting. Documentation of various kinds is often relevant to a criminal investigation. For example, a passport—is it genuine or false? Bank statements—is the individual deeply in debt or inexplicably rich? Finally, there is the possibility that evidence of criminality may also be found, such as drugs which may be irrelevant but could be central in a turf war between suppliers.

It is essential that all items recovered are labelled to maintain continuity (from crime scene to court) and suitably packaged to prevent contamination, minimize damage, and maximize the potential of recovering evidence. The packaging needs of different types of items varies hugely, and it is one of the main responsibilities of the CSM that this conforms to laboratory requirements. Packaging a wet, bloodstained item in the wrong way could result in contamination, cause the blood to degrade, and reduce the chance of DNA profiling. Failing to seal an item on which trace evidence could be found may result in it being excluded as evidence in a court hearing. The great variety in packaging is a consequence of the wide range of items that are encountered in investigations and the types of forensic tests available. The role of the CSI can be critical in giving guidance on packaging to maximize the chance of obtaining evidence and minimize adverse consequences. Although the details are very different, each type of packaging follows a number of relevant principles which include:

- protecting the item from the outside world by acting as a barrier to transfer of adventitious materials;
- preventing loss of material (especially trace evidence) from the item;
- protecting those handling and transporting the item from risk of injury, for example from broken glass or sharp weapons;
- protecting individuals from exposure to infectious agents (viruses, bacteria);
- allowing easy transport, handling, and storage.

Many aspects of scene management are procedural but it is essential at all times to consider the investigative implications of actions and decisions. The entire process must be thought through from beginning to end otherwise actions at one stage may compromise later possibilities. For example, swabbing a partial fingerprint in blood (to obtain a sample for DNA profiling) without advice from a fingerprint expert could compromise the outcome of the fingerprint examination. Such decisions need to be agreed and recorded as it may be necessary to justify them in court.

Forensic strategies

Asking the *correct* question is critical. I was once involved in a conversation along the following lines:

Q. Can you detect adrenaline that has been injected into someone who is dead?
A. I don't know—what is your hypothesis? Then we can work out how it can be tested.
Q. Have you seen *Pulp Fiction*...?

It is easy to fall into the trap of asking a question because there may be a scientific means of answering it rather than because it is the correct question to ask. To keep focused on relevant questions that may have scientific answers needs a realistic hypothesis about what may have happened. In *Pulp Fiction*, there is a scene in which John Travolta plunges an adrenaline-filled syringe into Uma Thurman's heart which instantly revives her. There is a degree of medical authenticity to the use of adrenaline in this way, but it is far from routine or free from danger. A problem in forensic science is that fictional events can gain currency in the real world; something that is commonly called the 'CSI effect'. In the investigation of a drug-related death, I was asked by the SIO if adrenaline could be detected in the body. I wasn't told anything else at that stage. Adrenaline is a natural substance that one would expect to find in the body, and unless there were huge amounts present it seemed to me unlikely that this was the most effective line of inquiry. Experienced forensic scientists know that these questions are a distraction from the real issues, since they are framed in the wrong way: as scientific questions as opposed to investigative ones. I replied that I didn't know (although I could have guessed) but also asked the SIO what he was trying to prove—this is how the question should have been framed. Only then was the *Pulp Fiction* scenario revealed. A much better approach is to formulate a hypothesis and identify scientific tests that might support or refute this. In the '*Pulp Fiction*' case, the hypothesis is that a syringe containing adrenaline has been plunged into someone's heart. How might we test this? Potential lines of inquiry might include:

- establishing if there were any witnesses (there were none, everyone was in a drugged stupor);
- looking for physical evidence of the event—syringes, ampoules of adrenaline (none were found as far as I was aware);
- testing samples from the body (if this is possible);
- examining the body to see if there is a needle-sized hole in the chest.

There are other possibilities, but of those suggested the examination of the body is quickest, simplest, most easily interpreted, and can be demonstrated to a jury or anyone else by means of a photograph. It gets my vote.

An SIO managing an investigation is surrounded by specialists and experts, police and otherwise. The SIO cannot know all the potential solutions and procedures, otherwise why would they need the other experts? Their primary role is to lead, coordinate, focus the inquiry on the key investigative issues, and resolve these by the best, quickest, and most efficient means possible. It is all too easy for imagination and pet theories to cause 'mission creep', but this can be avoided by using a small team to develop a forensic strategy which ensures constant focus on investigative issues and monitors progress regularly; daily in the early stages of a major investigation. The forensic management team also helps address another common problem. Many scientists do not fully understand the investigative methods used by the police, nor are they kept aware of the changing investigative priorities in an inquiry. Table 1 gives some indication of the complexity of this

Table 1. Crime types and forensic evidence. This table illustrates some general connections between particular types (or sources) of forensic evidence and crime types.

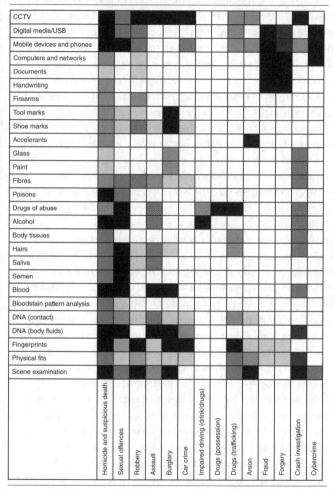

Key: Black—regular or routine; dark grey—occasionally or where relevant; light grey—rarely; blank—not applicable.

problem from the range of evidence types, and therefore disciplines and scientists who may be involved in a single case. As can be seen, although the investigation of homicide typically involves examination of body fluids and weapons, it can also involve almost any other type of evidence depending on the nature of the case and the issues that need to be proved, or eliminated. Sexual offences, assault, robbery, and investigation of vehicle crashes can also involve a wide range of different evidence types. DNA tends to be of most value in offences against the person, and fingerprints can be useful in almost any investigation. Some crimes, such as fraud, use a comparatively narrow range of evidence types (handwriting, documents, computer examination) and others, such as drink-driving, rely on a single type of evidence (quantification of alcohol). Although there is a general connection between crime types and the types of forensic evidence involved, every case is distinctive and there is a need to be alert to changing circumstances as well as unexpected, unusual and occasionally bizarre types of evidence. The following case illustrates some of these issues. Police attended the home of an elderly couple having been alerted by concerned neighbours. The body of the woman was found in her bed and she had been bound and gagged. Her husband was similarly restrained but still alive. I arrived at the scene late morning. There was no other information about the case at that time. The woman was wearing a nightgown which would be removed from her at the post mortem examination. As part of my examination I took tape lifts (or tapings) to recover trace evidence from the exposed parts of the body *in situ*, including her face and neck. I returned to the lab and looked at the tapings under a low power microscope without removing them from the transparent polythene bag I had sealed them into. On the tapes I could see what looked like tiny fragments of brown leather or suede. I contacted the investigation team to tell them I had completed my examination and asked if there was any more information about the case. It transpired that a man had been arrested in the early hours of the morning before the bodies had been found. He had been acting suspiciously and was now detained. It was possible he was connected to the murder but as yet there was no evidence of this. With the leather fragments in mind I asked what the man was wearing. The detective described the man's clothing and added as an afterthought that he had been carrying a bag in which he had a knife and a pair of brown suede gloves. (The knife was the reason why he had been arrested.) I asked for the gloves to be sent to the lab but didn't mention the leather fragments, it was too early for that. Before the gloves arrived I marked all the leather fragments on the tape so that they could be quickly removed. By late afternoon that day I had established that the brown suede fragments on the taping from the victim's neck matched the gloves in the detained man's bag.

From my training and general experience, I knew what leather fragments looked like microscopically but had never encountered leather traces in a case before. When I taped the woman's body I was recovering trace evidence and I anticipated that there might be fibres from her attacker present. When I looked at the tapes I was doing so out of curiosity; might there be something of interest there, something useful to the investigation? My phone call to the investigator was partly routine and partly investigative. I didn't mention the leather when I made the phone call because I didn't want to set any hares running.

In a further twist towards the end of the case I was told that the house was being released to the family of the victims. I was asked if I wanted to go back to the scene for anything while there was still an opportunity. Given that leather traces are so rarely encountered I wondered if there might be other sources in the house that matched the fragments from the body. To my surprise I found many swatches of leather and suede: the victim's hobby had been leather work. In all, I retrieved thirty-four samples, several of which were brown, but none of the brown samples matched the gloves.

Finally, to emphasize the point that there is no fixed formula for what could be evidence in a case, in the course of my career I have examined the following:

- 'raspberry sauce' (that vaguely resembled blood) and was used to write a threatening note;
- 'Sellotape' used to bind an alleged victim of a robbery (in fact the case was a set-up);
- a 'toxic' brown powder sent to Margaret Thatcher when she was Prime Minister (that was actually a gift of unusual spices);
- cabbage stalks, insects from a mausoleum, wooden fish forks, toilet paper, brocade curtains…

Need I go on? Yes, there is a pattern in many cases but one must always be alert to unpredictable opportunities.

It is sometimes more effective, quicker, or more convenient to bring the specialist to the crime scene. This is routine for crash investigation and fire investigation when the bulk of the examination takes place at the scene and is supported by follow-up laboratory work, but this is not typical of most other areas of forensic science. In both these areas, specialists are likely to be interested in events immediately prior to the incident and may also require information from eyewitnesses more readily available at the scene. The decision to call a specialist to a scene has to strike a balance between having another person at the scene who needs to be factored into the overall planning and the benefits of face-to-face discussions between the investigator and the expert. Shootings involving multiple deaths and fires involving loss of life or high-value property are likely to involve specialists at the scene. In the former, a pathologist and firearms expert working together can combine information from body positions, injuries, locations of spent cartridge cases, and bullet damage to surroundings, to reconstruct the incident. The main drawback of this approach is that the bodies must be left in position until the specialists complete their examination, which can present difficulties if the examination is protracted or the location is outdoors. An area of forensic biology which can be useful at the scene (and in the laboratory) is bloodstain pattern analysis (BPA). Information from this type of evidence can help reconstruct incidents, eliminate alternative explanations, and provide information about the sequence of events. Blood is a complex liquid that is a suspension of cells, proteins, salts, and enzymes. Blood droplets obey physical laws, and an understanding of these laws and how bloodstain patterns are created can allow scientists to interpret the crime scene. BPA requires an understanding of blood droplet dynamics and the expertise to link related blood patterns logically in light of other available information.

When force is applied to liquid blood, such as when a bleeding person is punched or struck with a weapon, the blood is dispersed as small droplets. The number and size of the droplets is related to various factors, including the force involved and the amount of blood present. Droplets can travel up to four metres from the point of impact and the distance travelled is related to their size: large droplets travel further than small ones. On landing, the droplets form a stain whose shape indicates the direction of travel and angle of impact. By triangulation using a number of droplets, it is possible to establish where the pattern originated from, and by inference, the location of the individual when the blow was struck. The angle of impact of each stain can be calculated by using the ratio of the width of the stain to its length, giving the sine of the angle. How to calculate the angle of impact and estimate the area of origin of bloodstains is illustrated in Figure 4. There are also a number of recognizable blood stain patterns which arise from specific events and can readily be identified. These are outlined in Table 2.

Not all bloodstain patterns are readily identifiable, and some patterns are fragmentary and difficult to interpret. The best patterns are usually found on smooth surfaces on stable or immovable light-coloured objects such as walls or heavy furniture. Items that

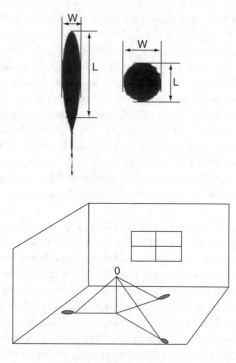

0 = area of origin of spatter

4. Calculating the angle of impact of bloodstains (top) and estimating the area of origin of blood spatter (bottom). The bloodstains above struck the surface at approximately 13° (top left) and 90° (top right).

can be moved or disturbed may not be in their original position and this may affect the interpretation. The analyst must think in three dimensions and try to establish logical links between patterns. At the same time, any contrary evidence which arises must be considered as this may indicate a better alternative explanation. The type of information that can be provided by BPA includes: the number and location of attack sites; sequence of attack and where it began; the positions of the victim and attacker during the incident; how close an individual was to the blood

Table 2. Characteristic bloodstain patterns. Interpreting these patterns in light of other information or evidence available can assist in reconstructing events at the crime scene.

Smear/ Contact	Indicates contact between a bloodstained item and another surface.
Drip	Free-falling blood droplets. A linear pattern indicates a trail.
Impact	A radial pattern of predominantly minute stains (around 1 mm) caused by force dispersing the blood. Generally correlated with violence.
Arterial	A distinctive pattern caused by blood escaping from a damaged artery.
Cast off (in-line)	A linear pattern of stains caused by blood being thrown from a moving object, typically a weapon such as a hammer.

spatter; if the body has been moved following the attack. The outcome of such an examination is subjective and rarely conclusive, but it can still be useful in certain types of offences such as homicides which involve blunt trauma and considerable bloodshed.

In 1996 a man attacked the Russell family as they walked home from school in Kent. Lin Russell and her daughter Megan were killed, and Josie, her other daughter, was gravely injured. The bodies were found in a remote wooded area close to a single-track road. I examined the bloodstain patterns at the crime scene. I had two main questions in mind. First, were there any bloodstains that might have come from the offender? Second, was it possible to establish the sequence of events at the scene such as who had been attacked first and whether any of the bodies had been moved afterwards. I found a single small round bloodstain on one of the bodies that did not appear to fit in with the surrounding blood patterns. I thought this could be from the attacker; alternatively, it could have dripped from the weapon, which was thought to be a hammer. DNA analysis showed that the blood matched one of the victims, so the most likely explanation was that it dripped from a weapon. On the single-track road there were bloodstains in the form of a drip pattern. This allowed me to infer that the attacks had started on the track before being continued inside the wood. The bloodstain patterns also showed that some of the bodies had been moved during the course of the attacks but there were too many possibilities to be confident about the exact sequence. This kind of information is typical of what can be established by BPA. Michael Stone was convicted of these crimes in 1998 and, following appeal and re-trial, he was convicted again in 2001. The conviction of Stone was controversial at the time and remains so today. The case against him was circumstantial and the key evidence incriminating him came from a fellow prisoner who said Stone had confessed to him.

Good crime scene management is critical to the effective application of forensic science in criminal investigations. Failure to protect the crime scene, and to manage contamination and continuity of evidence, are likely to have major implications for an investigation and could preclude significant lines of inquiry. Identification of the relevant questions to be addressed and the formulation of specific hypotheses for scientific testing are essential. Leadership, communication, and teamwork are also important to ensure the right experts are addressing the relevant questions, at the scene and in the laboratory.

Chapter 4
Laboratory examination: search, recovery, analysis

We now move from the crime scene to the laboratory and the various stages of recovering, documenting, and analysing evidence. Some of the principles and processes will now be familiar to us as they reflect those applied at crime scenes. The new dimension is the specific application of scientific testing of case items and the range of scientific disciplines involved. In this chapter, we will cover the types of examinations carried out in particular case types, and the specific scientific and legal procedures required to meet the standards of criminal law.

Recovery of evidence

The modern forensic science laboratory contains an array of science and technology that is focused on providing answers and indicating valuable lines of inquiry in criminal cases. In addition to meeting formal scientific standards, it has to comply with legislation and legal procedures. This chapter outlines how items are examined, the techniques that are used to recover evidence, and the potential range of methods available for analysis. The importance of minimizing contamination, maintaining continuity (chain of custody), and quality assurance are also explained. There is no standard structure that all laboratories follow as this will depend on the type and number of examinations they carry out.

Some labs employ only a small number of people, others can be very large, containing many hundreds of staff. Some labs are part of police organizations, others are public sector or state organizations, and some are private commercial enterprises. In England and Wales, all the major forensic science laboratories are private companies. The privatization of these laboratories remains a matter of considerable debate in terms of whether this is in the interest of justice. Some suggest that this arrangement will inevitably lead to erosion of standards and a focus on profits to the detriment of justice. Others point to industries with very high technical standards, such as the airline industry, as evidence that private enterprise does not mean lower standards of science and technology. In recent years there has been growing evidence of a fragmented and uncertain infrastructure for forensic science provision in England and Wales. In 2012 the Forensic Science Service (FSS) was closed by the UK government because of its unsustainable financial position. The FSS, a former public sector organization that was in the process of being privatized, was the largest forensic science provider in the UK with a worldwide reputation in practice and research. There have been many other changes in the now completely privatized sector. Numerous laboratories have merged, some have gone out of business, and there has been a major scandal about data manipulation in one laboratory that may result in a criminal prosecution. Many police forces have 'in-sourced' forensic testing but some have failed to comply with the quality assurance regimes required of forensic science labs. For example, almost all police forces in England and Wales failed to meet the Forensic Science Regulators' deadline in 2018 for the accreditation of fingerprint examinations. It appears that few police organizations understand the nature or purpose of quality assurance standards in forensic examinations. In most other countries around the world, large-scale commercialization of forensic science is rare and instead tends to be in the form of small companies which provide more specialist types of evidence such as DNA profiling. In Scotland there is a single national public sector forensic science service that is independently accredited. There is a similar arrangement in Northern Ireland.

Whatever their funding basis, most medium-sized labs (say around a hundred staff) will have broadly similar structures based on the types of investigation they are involved in and the scientific disciplines that they need to do this work. Very few labs in the world, perhaps none, have the capability to carry out every forensic examination, and most seek to balance the skills they have with their users' needs. What follows is an overview of the scientific disciplines, departments, and case types found in a medium-sized laboratory. The first stage in most examinations is the recovery of evidence and is often carried out by an assistant under the supervision of a case-reporting scientist. This involves the initial examination of a wide range of items such as clothing and weapons, to recover evidence for further analysis using standard techniques: visual examinations, taping, and sweeping. The materials recovered during this stage will be analysed in various departments of the lab depending on the disciplines involved and the case type, and may include:

- Analysis, comparison, and identification of minute quantities of paint, glass, and other chemical traces in burglary, thefts of materials, and road traffic crashes;

- Shoe marks, tool marks, tyre marks, and manufacturing marks of various kinds from a wide range of crimes;

- Analysis and identification of drugs of abuse including synthetic and natural products and prescribed drugs in cases of possession, supply, and importation of drugs;

- Identification and quantification of alcohol, drugs, and poisons in body samples in drink-driving cases, and suspicious or sudden deaths;

- Identification and recovery of blood, semen, saliva in cases of violent and sexual assault;

- Genetic analysis of biological fluids, tissues, and stains by DNA profiling and related techniques in criminal cases including kinship testing;

- Comparison and identification of textile fibres in robbery, sexual assaults, and homicide;

- Examination of questioned documents, printing and inks in fraud and counterfeit cases—including contracts, wills, letters, passports, currency—to establish ownership or authenticity;

- Examination of handwriting to attribute or eliminate a putative author, or to connect documents that may have been written by the same author;

- Examination and test firing of pistols, rifles, military weapons, and related devices. Identification of gunshot residues (GSR);

- Data extraction and analysis from desktop computers, networks, and mobile devices (phones, tablets, SATNAV, etc.);

- Routine record photography and analysis of imaging devices, such as media from CCTV and still cameras;

- Comparison, identification, and enhancement of fingermarks. In most cases, the laboratory work is confined to enhancement of marks, with comparison being carried out in a separate fingerprint department.

The bulk of the work in most laboratories will be related to burglary, car crime, and drugs analysis, where small numbers of items will be examined in individual cases. Although serious offences will be small in number, these cases are more variable and more complex, and the workload is usually higher.

Before the examination there are some basic steps to take. The first is to ensure that you have all the available information to carry out an examination, including relevant witness statements and police reports. This usually means a phone call to the investigating officer to check if any facts may have changed (this can happen overnight in major cases). Some basic planning needs to take place to ensure you have identified an appropriate sequence of examinations, for example, you can't look for the red fibres from the jumper of the victim until you know what these look like.

This of course raises an issue of potential contamination, so you need to make sure that all relevant examinations are separated in space (different benches in different labs) and time (different days) and by wearing different protective clothing. If there are three suspects, two victims, and a scene involved in a case, this will take some careful thought and planning. The risks of contamination are higher given that all of the materials from the incident are now in one place (the laboratory) and will probably be examined by a single scientist. However, the items are now in controlled conditions and can be managed more easily and effectively than at a crime scene. From the outset, systematic, stringent procedures are taken to prevent contamination, and records that demonstrate compliance with these procedures are made and retained. What constitutes contamination and the steps taken to avoid it varies in the different disciplines of forensic science, and to an extent in different laboratories. Trace evidence—glass, paint, soil, hairs, fibres, and DNA (contact DNA)—is particularly prone to contamination, and the following steps are commonly used to minimize this. Items from different sources, for example the scene, suspect, and victim, are stored from the outset of the examination in separate places. The sequence of the examination should minimize the contamination risk. Where possible the trace evidence is recovered *before* the control sample (the potential source) is examined. Once the traces are recovered, the opportunities for contamination are considerably lower. Items from which trace evidence is to be recovered are examined in different locations and at different times, generally a minimum of a working day apart.

Different lab coats, examination benches, and instruments are used for each related set of items, for example a set of clothing from one individual. Extensive use is made of disposable instruments and disposable protective clothing. The instruments assigned to a search bench are dedicated to it and do not leave it. The lab coat used is stored there until the case is finished. All of the above details are noted in the case file.

On 15 July 1992, Rachel Nickell was murdered in broad daylight on Wimbledon Common, London. The case remained unsolved for many years largely due to police incompetence and bias. In 2004, a DNA profile was found on samples from Rachel's body and a DNA database search linked the profile to a man called Robert Napper. At the time Napper was detained in Broadmoor hospital, a secure psychiatric institution in England. He had been convicted of the double murder of Jacqueline Bissett and her daughter Jasmine in horrific circumstances, as well as a number of rapes. The cases that Napper had been convicted of were examined in the same laboratory and by the same scientist (unknowingly) as the Nickell case. In fact, items stained with semen that matched Napper had been examined on the same day and on the same bench as the item from Nickell on which the DNA profile was found. Items stained with body fluids matching Napper were also stored in the same cupboard as the item from Nickell on which the DNA profile was found. The crucial question about the DNA in the Nickell case was whether it was present due to contamination or whether it was indeed evidence that Napper was the killer. I was asked to review the case by the Metropolitan Police to answer this question. It was a long and detailed review that took into account laboratory procedures and analyses in all of the cases that Napper had been involved in. This included the detailed tracking and movements of hundreds of individual items in the cases over a period of fourteen years: where they had been stored in numerous police stations and labs; who had handled them; and evaluation of the significance of the DNA results that had been obtained. It was impossible for me to exclude the possibility of contamination, but my opinion was that the most likely explanation was that the DNA had been transferred to Nickell when she was attacked by Napper.

Examination of items

In this section, we consider mainly biological evidence while other types of evidence (DNA, fingerprints, traces, drugs, toxicology,

GSR) are covered in later chapters. The general principles of how to search for, recover, and record biological evidence also apply to many of these other types of evidence although the details will vary, particularly the way in which different types of evidence are analysed.

The examination of clothing for body fluids, such as blood, and trace evidence would commence on a clean bench. The examiner will wear a disposable lab coat, gloves, face mask, and cap. The tools used in the examination (pens, forceps, etc.) will be located at that bench and will not be removed from there. The examination of an individual item proceeds as follows. Check and note the label and compare with the relevant paperwork. There should be no significant discrepancies. Review the integrity of the packaging. The item should be sealed and the packaging intact. Any deficiencies, such as damage or poor seals, must be noted.

Scan the item briefly for visible material of interest that might be easily dislodged and lost. This should be removed and retained in a separate labelled package. Minimal handling should occur at this stage. If required, the surface of the item is then taped using transparent adhesive tape to recover extraneous trace evidence. Tapes from each item are packaged separately and labelled with the item details. Slowly and systematically visually examine the item for other relevant evidence. Describe the item—a shoe, jumper, or knife—in sufficient detail for it to be identified readily in future, for example in court. Note its condition (old, new, worn), and any other significant or distinguishing features such as stains, marks, or damage. In cases where items subsequently may be searched for fibres matching the item being examined, a control sample should be removed. This must be representative of the item and include all fibre types and colours. The case notes should reflect what an item was examined for, its description, and any findings and interpretations, accurately and concisely, supported by measurements, diagrams, and photographs where relevant.

The purpose of examining items in this manner is to ensure that all evidence is recovered; to identify any relevant materials, such as body fluids, present; to produce accurate, detailed notes; and to determine which analyses will be carried out next. These notes will be continually updated throughout the examination of the case and act as a detailed history of events and information received as well as analytical results. For example, if a case briefing is held, a record of the meeting will be stored in the case file. The case file will subsequently be used as the basis for legal reports and to act as an aide-memoire when giving evidence in court.

Blood and body fluids

In physical and sexual assaults, body fluids can be shed and transferred to clothing, objects, and weapons. In addition to identifying the source, that is the individual from whom the stain has come, the location, amount, and pattern of staining can be important in interpreting findings. A common explanation for bloodstaining found on the clothing of individuals accused of assault is that they were near the attack but did not take part in it. The staining therefore must be examined to determine if there is any evidence to support or refute this. Saliva staining inside a mask can indicate that it has been worn and by whom. Semen and saliva are also routinely encountered in sexual offences on body swabs (e.g. from the vagina) and clothing, particularly underwear. Locating and identifying blood, semen, saliva, and other biological materials forms a routine aspect of forensic biology.

The first stage of the examination uses a number of simple tests (so-called presumptive tests) that can give an initial indication of the type of stain which is then further analysed by confirmatory tests. Dried bloodstains have a characteristic red-brown appearance and are usually easily recognizable. A number of presumptive tests, for example the Kastle Meyer (KM) test, can be used to indicate the presence of blood. This test relies on catalytic activity of haemoglobin, the protein found in red blood cells. Blood causes the oxidation by peroxidase of the colourless form of phenolphthalein to give a bright pink colour. The combination of the visual appearance of the bloodstain followed by a satisfactory KM test is generally regarded as sufficient to establish that a stain is blood. Stains that give a KM positive test but do not resemble blood may be mixtures of blood with another body fluid, such as saliva due to bleeding from the mouth. Alternatively, the stain may not contain blood, as other biological materials and some chemical oxidants can give false positive reactions, although these are rare. The test is applied by taking a small piece of filter paper and rubbing it gently against the stain. Since DNA profiles can be successfully obtained from extremely small stains, one must ensure that the stain is not lost or destroyed in this process.

Semen consists of a fluid (seminal plasma) containing many millions of sperm as well as proteins, salts, sugars, and ions. Seminal staining on fabrics is usually whitish in colour but this can vary, especially if it is mixed with other body fluids. It can also form deposits that are colourless so can be difficult to locate on some items. Establishing the presence of seminal staining relies on detecting seminal fluid and sperm. Seminal fluid contains a high concentration of the enzyme acid phosphatase (AP) that can be detected using a presumptive test known as the AP, or brentamine, test. This test relies on the formation of a purple azo dye from brentamine due to the catalytic action of AP. The deeper the colour and the faster it appears (usually a few seconds), the more confident one can be that the reactions are due to seminal fluid. Other body fluids, in particular vaginal fluid, can also react to this test but the colour is different (more pinkish) and the reaction takes longer (over thirty seconds). However, given that most stains encountered in sexual offences are mixtures of semen and vaginal fluid, the difficulties in interpreting such a test will be evident. Following a strong AP test, the presence of sperm can identify semen. This is done by microscopic examination of a small amount

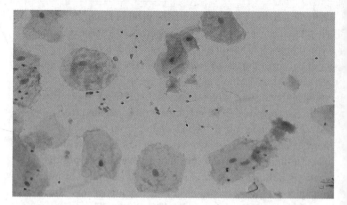

5. **Sperm and vaginal cells stained with haematoxylin and eosin.**

of material extracted from the stain. Sperm have a characteristic appearance (see Figure 5), consisting of a head and tail section, and can be stained using histological dyes. The amount of semen found on vaginal swabs can be used to estimate time since intercourse, although this method is fairly crude.

Saliva is encountered in sexual offences and other cases, such as robberies (on masks and gags) and homicides. Saliva is secreted by the salivary glands and contains water, mucus, proteins, salts, and enzymes. One of the enzymes present—amylase—is found in very high concentrations compared to other body fluids, and its detection can indicate the presence of saliva. Saliva deposits usually form colourless stains, therefore identification must consider the circumstances and location of the stain. The presence of epithelial cells typical of those from the mouth can sometimes be used as a confirmatory test, but these cells are similar to those found in the vagina (and elsewhere in the body) and are therefore of limited value.

The tests described above usually constitute the first steps in cases involving biological evidence, but the scientific procedures in a major case will require extensive examinations by other scientific disciplines with the aim of establishing answers to investigative inquiries.

Table 3 provides a summary of the types of examination carried out in laboratories and the range of analytical techniques involved. Although many specialist techniques are used, we can say that in almost all instances the process begins with a visual examination of the items involved, usually to recover the evidence. The most commonly used range of techniques is microscopy, of which there are a number of specialist types that have particular application for the examination and comparison of trace evidence. Presumptive testing is also widely used to screen biological and chemical substances. The main analytical method which underpins most forensic biology work is DNA profiling, since this can identify the donor of almost any type of biological fluid or tissue.

A large number of analytical techniques are used to identify the diverse range of substances encountered in forensic chemistry. The particular method used will depend on the nature of the substance involved, whether it is organic or inorganic, solid or liquid, or present in trace quantities or large amounts. Some of these techniques are described in Chapter 7 (trace evidence), and Chapter 8 (drugs and toxicology). It is not possible to cover all of the techniques in the table, but for those readers who wish to explore this area further, suitable references are provided.

Physical fits

This chapter is about the recovery and analysis of evidence, but on occasions both of these processes can be remarkably simple. A physical fit occurs when two separate items fit together in a way that it is (often instantly) recognizable that they were originally one item. This rarely requires any analytical equipment other than occasionally a low-power microscope, nor does it require any scientific interpretation. For example, a twenty-four-hour service

Table 3. Analytical methods for different types of evidence.

Method	Fingerprints	Blood	Semen	Saliva	Hairs	Fibres	Paint	Glass	Drugs	Poisons	Colour and dyes	Polymers and plastics	Gunshot residues	Metals and minerals	Soil	Flammable liquids
Refractive index								█								
SEM													█	█	█	
X-ray microprobe														█	█	
X-ray Diffraction														█	█	
FTIR						▒	█		█			█				
Pyrolysis GC (-MS)							█									
GC-MS									█	█		█				
LC-MS									▒	█						
Mass spectrometry (MS)												█				
Gas chromatography																█
HPLC																
Thin layer Chromatography							▒		█		█					
Microspectrophotometry						█	█									
UV/visible spectrometry									█	█						
DNA sequencing			█		█											
DNA profiling		█	█	█												
Presumptive tests		█	█	░					█							
Comparison microscopy							█	█	█							
Polarized light microscopy						█	█	▒				█			█	
High power microscopy			█	▒	█	█										
Low power microscopy		▒	░		█	█	█					█				
Ultra-violet light/laser	█	░	░			█						█				
Visual examination	█								█	█	█		█	█	█	█

Key: Black—regular or routine; dark grey—occasionally or where relevant; light grey—rarely; blank—not applicable.

station in London was robbed and the assistant was handed a McDonald's takeaway bag to put the cash in. As the robber took the bag, the assistant held on to it, gently tearing a small piece off. The fragment contained parts of the multi-coloured McDonald's logo and fitted perfectly with the torn section of the bag recovered from the robber's address. A photograph of the items fitting together as one was taken to accompany the short statement and to illustrate the nature and significance of the evidence. A similar example to this is illustrated in Figure 6. In a second example, fragments of glass from a broken container and a piece of burnt fabric were recovered from the scene of a fire and were suspected to be parts of a petrol bomb. The glass fragments pieced together to form most of a milk bottle and the fabric was a badly burnt fragment from a white vest which bore traces of a flammable liquid. The remains of a white vest were recovered from a suspect's premises and were compared with the burnt fragment. In this case, the match was less clear-cut and required careful microscopic examination of both the vest and burnt fragment to establish a fit. Nonetheless, the burnt fragment fitted together with part of the left shoulder strap of the vest, showing that they were originally one item.

Until now, we have been considering the process of examination, the physical actions and logical steps by which it is achieved. There is a great deal more to an effective examination than following a process. In searching, there is a need to be alert to potential evidence that may be unforeseen. The examiner must take an intelligent, inquiring approach which is suitably detached and dispassionate. It is reasonable to have general expectations—we know that individuals involved in violence where there has been bloodshed may get blood on their clothing—but we should not be motivated by such expectations in individual cases to achieve any particular outcome. We proceed from observation to analysis and then by inference to interpretation. Statements and reports should also follow this pattern as we move from observation (fact), analysis (fact), interpretation (a mixture of fact and opinion), to

ASDA Stores Ltd. Leeds, LS11 5AD

Blantyre   13:18
Merchant No. 28799503
** SALE **

PUMP 6   Unleaded
Terminal No. 21301856
20.02 L   @   99.9 P /L.
= GBP20. 00

TOTAL /GBP20. 00

VISA DEBIT ************
Expiry Date 06/14
Auth Code
Verified by Pin

AID: A0009000031010

Total includes VAT @ 15.0%
VAT NO 362 0127 92

6. Physical fit of two parts of a petrol receipt.

conclusion (usually opinion). A report should separate fact and
opinion so that this is clear to the reader. The discipline of this
procedure is valuable; otherwise we can be prone to errors that
arise from statements which are opinion but appear to be fact. In
other words, the sequence is not only procedural but cognitive.
Considerable care is needed to prevent the synthesis of fact and

interpretation in our minds because we are so used to handling particular types of analyses and interpretations. For example, we categorize a blood pattern as 'impact' on the basis of an inference from our observation of certain characteristics. This is nonetheless a contestable assertion and not a fact, an assertion we need to explain, justify, and defend if necessary. Much of the value of forensic science derives from the combination of scientific testing and rational transparent process which can be judged by others as objective (or not). It is the scientific approach that is objective, not the scientists: scientists are no more objective than anyone else.

This chapter has covered the fundamental processes of forensic examination: search, recovery, and analysis. It has also described the range of methods involved in such analyses, how to prevent contamination and maintain the integrity of the evidence, and some of the issues that arise in the interpretation of evidence. In the following chapters, we will consider these issues and other specific areas of forensic science in more detail.

Chapter 5
DNA profiling and databases

In 1984, the body of 17-year-old Melanie Road was found 300 yards from her home in Bath. She had been stabbed and sexually assaulted. A long blood trail extended from her body which was examined by a forensic scientist. The scientist established that there were, in fact, two intermingled blood trails not just one. Blood grouping matched one of the trails to Melanie and the other to an unknown person. Further investigations by the police at the time failed to identify the murderer. In 1996, a DNA profile was produced from the unknown blood and the National DNA database was searched but no match was identified. The case was continually reviewed and the DNA profile upgraded in line with new scientific developments. A DNA profile was also developed from semen found on Melanie's trousers. A 'cold case' review team was set up to monitor the case, and in 2014 a 'familial' match to the crime profile was obtained. Familial searching relies on the fact that related individuals share a much larger proportion of their DNA than unrelated individuals. A parent and child share at least half of their genetic markers. Investigators began to screen relatives of the matching individual with the aim of identifying an offender. In 2014, Christopher Hampton was sampled as part of this screen and his DNA matched the semen profile from Melanie's trousers and the blood trail. Hampton initially denied the offence but later pleaded guilty to murder.

In not much more than thirty years, the law has moved from considering DNA profiling as usurping the role of the jury to fully embracing it as a distinctive and positive contribution to the investigation and prosecution of crime. DNA profiling has also set a new standard for forensic evidence, sometimes referred to as the 'gold standard'. This is because it is more reliable and robust than any other type of forensic evidence. The reliability of DNA testing derives from the fact that it has followed a traditional path from discovery to application typical of new scientific developments, and the evidence for this has been published, peer reviewed, and challenged in the scientific community. Many other areas of forensic evidence do not live up to the new standards set by DNA testing, as we will later see.

The discovery of DNA profiling by Sir Alec Jeffreys in the mid-1980s was the single most important breakthrough in the investigation of crime since the discovery of fingerprints and, amongst other things, led to the establishment in England of the world's first DNA database, in 1995. The impact of DNA profiling has been immense because it can eliminate or identify an individual, from minute traces 'invisible' to the naked eye, with great confidence. This chapter explains the structure of DNA, the mechanism of DNA profiling, how it is interpreted, and the operation of DNA databases.

DNA and the human genome

DNA is the genetic material of most living organisms and plays a central role in determining hereditary characteristics. DNA is a major component of the chromosomes found in the nucleus of each cell in the body and is also found in cell organelles called mitochondria (mitochondrial DNA (mtDNA)). DNA consists of two complementary chains of molecules wound around each other in the form of a double helix. Each chain consists of molecules of the sugar deoxyribose linked by phosphate molecules. Attached to each sugar is one of four nitrogenous bases: adenine (A), thymine (T), guanine (G), and cytosine (C), to form a nucleotide. The relationship between pairs of these nucleotides is the basis for the complementary chain, in that adenine only pairs with thymine and guanine only with cytosine. This means that when the chains separate for replication each can form a complementary version of the other, resulting in two identical molecules. The diagram in Figure 7 illustrates the structure of DNA and the relationship between DNA and other parts of the cell.

Human cells have twenty-two pairs of matched (or homologous) chromosomes and a pair of sex chromosomes (XX, female; or XY, male) that make up the genome, the entire complement of genetic

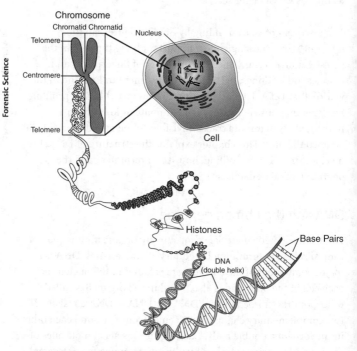

7. **The structure of DNA, its relationship with chromosomes, and location within the cell.**

material. Each chromosome consists of a single continuous strand of DNA, together with proteins known as histones that support the organization and packaging of the DNA. A child inherits one of each pair of chromosomes from their parents. Genes are found at different locations (loci) on each chromosome and consist of two copies called alleles. Only about 1.5 per cent of nuclear DNA is involved in the expression and regulation of genes. The remainder of the genome does not appear to play a role in gene expression and contains what is referred to as non-coding DNA. The non-coding parts of the genome contain large amounts of repetitive DNA sequences, of which short tandem repeats (STRs) are the most important in DNA profiling. Non-coding DNA is inherited in the same way as the rest of the genome. In STRs, the core repeat element is typically between one and six base pairs. Different alleles will have different numbers of repeats of the core sequence, and there are thousands of STRs scattered throughout the human genome. The most useful STRs consist of different numbers of tetranucleotides (sets of four nucleotides) that form each allele and occur in particular frequencies in human populations. It is from this variation that the power of DNA profiling arises. Because we know these alleles are inherited independently from one another, their frequencies can be multiplied together to determine how common each combination of alleles (the DNA profile) is in the population.

Analysis of DNA

The first step in this process is the extraction and purification of the DNA. The method for this varies depending on the tissue or stain type involved, and some tissues, such as epithelial cells, are easier to deal with than others, such as bone. In this process, cell membranes are disrupted, proteins are denatured, and the DNA is separated from the denatured protein. A particular process of extraction is required for stains containing semen and semen mixed with epithelial cells from body fluids such as vaginal fluid or saliva. This process is known as differential extraction and relies on the fact that sperm are resistant to the enzyme that breaks down cell membranes and require the addition of a reducing agent to break down the wall of the sperm. Following extraction, it is important to quantify the amount of DNA that has been recovered, as this can vary widely and the amount used in the next stage of the process is important. Between 0.2 nanograms (10^{-9} grams) and 1.0 nanograms of DNA is needed for optimum results.

DNA can be amplified for analysis using the polymerase chain reaction (PCR) and quantified in 'real time'. The PCR process (Figure 8) results in an exponential increase in the amount of targeted DNA (i.e. the DNA in the alleles being analysed) being amplified and explains why profiles can be obtained from such tiny samples. At full efficiency, thirty-two cycles of the PCR produce over eight billion copies. Two short pieces of synthetic DNA known as primers are required to flank the target DNA to identify it. The design of these primers ensures that only target human DNA and not that from other species is amplified.

STRs used for forensic purposes are selected on the basis that the alleles involved are:

- not linked to other genes such as those influencing physical characteristics or those associated with inherited disorders;
- inherited independently of each other;
- small and stable, so being comparatively resistant to degradation by heat, moisture, bacterial action, etc.;
- highly discriminating due to the high level of variation exhibited.

Analysis takes place in multiplexes, that is, many tests are carried out at the same time in the same test tube. DNA 17 is the most common DNA profiling method currently used in European forensic labs. Another analysis kit, DNA 24, which contains more tests, is used in Scotland and some US states. The DNA 17 kit is

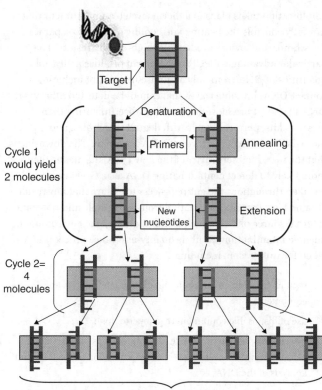

Target

Denaturation

Cycle 1
would yield
2 molecules

Primers   Annealing

New
nucleotides   Extension

Cycle 2 =
4
molecules

Cycle 3 = 8 molecules

8. The polymerase chain reaction. At the end of each cycle of heating and cooling the amount of DNA present doubles.

produced by three manufacturers to agreed standards and tests sixteen DNA sites (thirty-two alleles) and one sex marker. The DNA 24 kit includes all of the loci in the DNA 17 kit as well as a number of additional loci and uses the same number of amplification cycles (twenty-nine). Both systems are compatible with the European Standard (loci) Set and with CODIS (Combined DNA Index System) used in the USA. The process of amplification takes place in a thermocycler, an instrument that carefully controls the heating and cooling of DNA to separate the strands and ensure predictable, high-quality results. The particular advantage of PCR is that it can produce analysable quantities of DNA from only a minuscule amount including contact DNA, invisible traces that cannot be detected otherwise. DNA 17 and 24 are more sensitive and discriminating than previous kits, perform better with degraded samples, and are more likely to detect mixtures of DNA if present. The downside is that the increased sensitivity of the new DNA kits means they are more likely to detect contaminating DNA also. Great care needs to be taken throughout the entire process to ensure that any result obtained is a true one originating from the sample and not some external source of DNA, such as the analyst or the environment, due to contamination. Routine quality-assurance procedures are taken for this reason, including:

- regular cleaning and decontamination of laboratories and equipment;

- use of disposable equipment (e.g. pipette tips);

- wearing disposable protective clothing, such as masks and mob caps, by analysts at all stages in the examination of the item and analysis of the DNA;

- separate, dedicated laboratories, equipment, and work streams for the handling of reference materials (i.e. those known to have come from suspects, witnesses, or victims) and crime samples;

- use of independently accredited methods of analysis and standard operating procedures that include positive and negative controls in each test run;

- maintenance of staff (police, CSIs, scientists) and supplier (e.g. kit manufacturers) databases for investigation of contamination events.

Together, these steps minimize the chances of contamination and maximize the likelihood of discovering contamination should it occur. To reduce the risk of misleading results most labs will check the DNA profile obtained against a database that includes forensic staff and police to eliminate individuals who were involved in sample collection, examination, and analysis. There is a perception that DNA profiling is an entirely scientific process exclusively carried out in labs. This is not so. All DNA profiling relies on a complex network of often unseen individuals from cleaners to forensic medical examiners, and organizations from consumable suppliers to sophisticated laboratories.

On 25 April 2007, a police officer was murdered in Heilbronn, Germany. A long investigation ensued involving over a hundred police officers and prosecutors that connected this case to six other murders in France, Germany, and Austria between 1993 and 2009. The crucial link between all of the cases was a female DNA profile. The DNA was found on a cup in the murder of a 61-year-old woman, on a kitchen drawer in the home of a murdered man, in a car used to dispose of the bodies of three men, and in the car of a murdered nurse. There was no other evidence in these cases; no eyewitnesses, no CCTV, no fingerprints. The ensuing media frenzy dubbed the mysterious female serial killer 'the Phantom of Heilbronn'. A puzzling aspect of the investigation was DNA links to other offences: robberies, break-ins, stolen cars and motorbikes, and the theft of a toy pistol. Not only was the gender of the killer unusual (female serial killers are very rare) but the pattern of offences was very odd also. Some investigators had doubts about whether all of these cases were truly linked and when a matching DNA profile was obtained from the burned body of an asylum seeker in 2009, there was a strong suggestion that the results were spurious. At the time most DNA samples were removed from items using cotton swabs made specifically for this purpose. The swabs were sterile, meaning they did not carry any infectious agents, but that did not mean there was no DNA present. An investigation revealed that the swabs had been contaminated when they were being manufactured and packed, and the DNA profile of the mysterious phantom could be linked to women in the manufacturing plant. This was not the only manufacturer of these swabs in Europe but all of the linked cases used swabs from this source. Police organizations and labs who used other manufacturers were not affected. Swabs for DNA analysis must now be guaranteed to be DNA free and are routinely checked for trace DNA contamination.

DNA experts carry out the analysis and statistical evaluation of DNA, but the integrity of this analysis relies on many others who are involved before the samples arrive at the laboratory. It is also worth remembering that the ultimate interpretation of DNA evidence is made by a judge or a jury. And this interpretation is also dependent on how the case is presented in court by advocates who may have opposing views of what the DNA means. The ultimate meaning of any DNA evidence depends not only on the experts but on those who are called to adjudicate the evidence of a case as a whole.

Analysis and interpretation of DNA profiles

Different alleles in DNA profiles vary in molecular weight and can therefore be analysed by the technique of electrophoresis. This separates molecules on the basis of their electrical charge and mass. There are many different types of electrophoresis, but the most widely used method for DNA analysis is capillary gel electrophoresis. Coloured dyes are attached to the DNA and these are detected by a laser to produce an electropherogram (EPG) similar to that shown in Figures 9 and 10. The peaks in the EPG represent the alleles detected. Some of the peaks indicated are size markers: fragments of DNA of known size to allow calculation of the allele sizes in the profile. From left to right on the EPG, the DNA fragments represented are larger and therefore more prone to degradation. There are also tiny peaks near the bigger peaks due to artefacts which can be safely ignored for our purposes. The first figure illustrates kinship testing using ten loci (twenty alleles) and a sex marker (amelogenin). Each locus consists of two alleles,

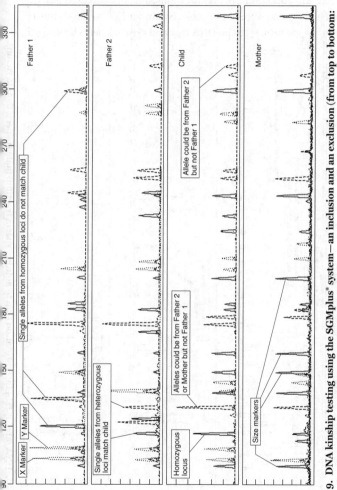

9. DNA kinship testing using the SGMplus® system—an inclusion and an exclusion (from top to bottom: alleged father 1, alleged father 2, child, mother).

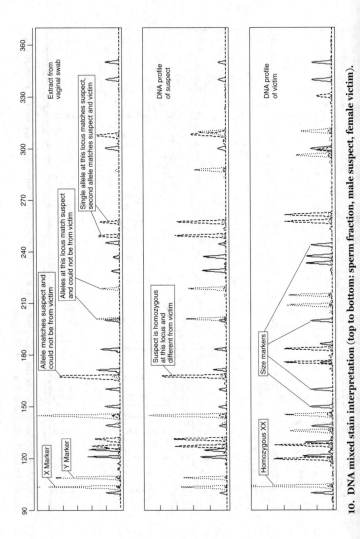

10. DNA mixed stain interpretation (top to bottom: sperm fraction, male suspect, female victim).

and when they are different (heterozygous), which is often the case, two peaks will be seen in the EPG. Where the same allele is inherited from each parent (homozygous), only one peak will be detected which will be taller due to the increased signal from the two identical alleles.

In Figure 9, four DNA profiles can be seen—from top to bottom, possible father 1, possible father 2, child (a son), and mother. At the far left of each profile, the dotted peaks indicate the sex of the donor—two peaks (from the X and Y chromosomes) for the three males and a single homozygous peak (XX) from the mother. Unless there has been mutation (which is very rare but is factored into any comparison), all of the alleles in the child's profile must have come from either the mother or father. As we move from left to right, the first peak (solid line) in the child's EPG shows he is homozygous for this locus. The mother shows two peaks at this position and so is heterozygous. One of these alleles matches the child, as would be expected. If we consider the EPGs from the putative fathers, father 2 is heterozygous and one of these alleles matches the child; father 1 is homozygous but the allele is different from the child's (the single peak is in a slightly different position). This indicates that father 2 could be the true biological father and provides the first indication that father 1 may not be. The next peaks in the EPG are dashes, representing a second locus. The first large dashed peak at the left of the child's EPG indicates he is homozygous at this locus, as is the mother. Father 2 is heterozygous and one of the alleles matches, therefore he must be included at this stage. Father 1 is homozygous but has a different allele, and this further supports the contention that he is not the true father. This process is continued until every locus has been compared, and at each stage evidence accumulates that father 1 is different (at six loci) and that father 2 could be the true father. Following the analysis, a calculation of the probability of father 2 being the biological father of the child compared to any male in the local population can be reported.

The second example is typical of a DNA profile obtained from a stain in a sexual offence. In most cases, such stains come from mixtures of body fluids from the parties involved, typically semen, vaginal secretions, and/or saliva. If this is not established from the initial analysis of the stain, the presence of a mixture may be inferred from the fact that there are more than two alleles at any one locus, or from the location where the stain was found, such as on the skin or clothing of the victim. In this case, the DNA profile comes from staining on a vaginal swab taken from the victim of an alleged rape. The top EPG is from a differential extraction of semen from the swab, the middle one is from the suspect, and the bottom EPG from the victim. DNA from the cells of the victim will be found on the swab, and the purpose of differential extraction is to obtain as much DNA from any sperm as possible while leaving behind that from the vaginal cells. This can be achieved because the sperm is more resistant to the enzyme used to break down the cells and can then be separated by centrifugation. This process does not always completely work and sometimes a mixed profile is obtained. To interpret this profile some assumptions have to be made. The main one is that any alleles found which match the donor are from the donor, and that only alleles which differ from the donor can be reliably attributed to another individual. It is clear that the DNA in the stain is from a male, since both the X and Y markers have been detected. By comparing the EPG from the stain with that of the victim, you will see that there are peaks which could not have originated from the victim, some of which are indicated. If these peaks are then compared with the profile from the alleged offender, you will see that these match this individual. There are other peaks present which are shared by each of the individuals involved. In summary, DNA has been found on the vaginal swab from the victim which could not be from the victim and matches the alleged offender. The question then becomes: what is the significance of this?

The sensitivity of the newest DNA analysis kits also means that they detect more mixtures, some of which can be complex, containing several individuals. A further complicating factor is that background DNA from the environment is also sometimes detected. Background DNA does not come from a single individual but from different people who have left traces. Interpreting mixtures is considerably more complex and subjective than interpreting single DNA profiles, and there are different philosophies and protocols for this purpose. Many factors are common to the different approaches including: identifying individual peaks and separating true peaks from background DNA and deciding which combinations of peaks are most likely. There is now software available to aid interpretation that reduces some of the subjective judgements involved. Whatever the approach, interpretation needs to be done before reference samples are considered by the analyst to avoid any bias that might occur.

Assessing the significance of an unmixed profile can be done in different ways using the frequency of the profile. This requires understanding of population genetics and statistics that allow estimation of allele frequencies and hence genotypes. This takes into account issues such as population size, chance of co-ancestry, and sample size. Since the alleles that lead to the genotypes are independently inherited, the frequency of the profile is the product of the individual genotypes. An example from a straightforward unmixed profile is illustrated in Table 4. The chance of two unrelated people sharing this profile, the match probability, is the reciprocal of the profile frequency and in this case is 1 in 1.4×10^{12}. So a matching DNA profile can be used to attribute body fluids or tissues to an individual with great confidence.

Evaluating evidence

One of the reasons why DNA provides such powerful numerical evidence is that it combines two of the most important elements of science. First, it uses empirical data about the world around us, in this case about population genetics and relationships between

Table 4. DNA genotype frequencies. For the purpose of illustration, the frequencies for father 2 in the example above have been used.

Locus	Genotype	Genotype frequency
D19S433	14, 14	0.129
D3S1358	17, 17	0.032
D8S1179	14, 14	0.256
VWA	17, 17	0.073
THO1	9, 9.3	0.077
D21S11	30, 30	0.053
FGA	21, 22	0.058
D16S539	11, 14	0.081
D18S51	15, 18	0.024
D2	20, 20	0.020
Complete profile	All of the above	7.09×10^{-13}

people. Second, these data are interpreted using objective statistical methods. As individuals, we are constantly making judgements but it is well known that our subjective judgements and assessments of probabilities are flawed in many instances. Furthermore, our judgements are subject to certain innate biases. An understanding of statistical probability highlights some of these flaws. A good example of our poor ability to estimate probabilities is the 'gambler's dilemma'. Following a long run of red in a roulette game, what should we bet on the next spin of the wheel? Many people believe subjectively that black is more likely, but since each spin of the wheel is independent of the previous one, the probability for black or red remain the same. A similar issue can occur with the tossing of a coin. We tend to see what we consider to be a pattern from a very short run of tosses that are statistically insignificant—say four heads in a row. Again, the odds of obtaining a head or a tail remain the same. These dangers also apply to the interpretation of forensic evidence, and so it is much better to rely on statistical probabilities than our subjective judgements. Paul Kirk considered probability to be the 'keynote of the interpretation of all physical evidence'.

There are different ways of estimating the significance of DNA profiles, such as the profile frequency (how often it is likely to be found in a given population) or the match probability (the reciprocal of the frequency), which both give a guide. However, there are difficulties with frequencies, and match probabilities also have their limitations. One of these difficulties is that when the number is very small it can be easily misunderstood. How does one interpret a match probability of one in a billion with reference to the UK population, which is around sixty-six million? A second difficulty is that a very small match probability in relation to a person who is innocent can be misinterpreted as implying that the person is guilty. This misinterpretation is known as the 'prosecutor's fallacy', or transposed conditional. Another statistical way of evaluating evidence used for DNA profiles is based on a theory invented by the Reverend Thomas Bayes, in 1764, which uses a ratio of probabilities called the likelihood ratio. In the context of forensic science, the important probabilities are the probability of the evidence if the prosecution's proposition is true (the person is guilty) and the probability of the evidence if the defence proposition is true (the person is innocent).

Bayesian evaluation of evidence avoids some of the difficulties encountered when the relative frequency of the evidence is used. This can be illustrated using a well-known theoretical example. Suppose a rape has been committed in a town where there are 10,000 men, and where for other reasons we can be confident one of them committed the crime. From the crime scene, traces of minerals are found which connect the offender to a local mine where 200 men work. When a suspect is arrested, similar traces are found on his clothing. What is the significance of this evidence? To illustrate this case, we need to assume that all of the men in the mine will have similar mineral traces on them.

Although this is not necessarily the case, let us say it is valid for the purpose of this illustration. There are 9,999 men in the town who are innocent and 199 of them work in the mine. We can estimate the probability of finding this evidence on an innocent man as 199/9,999: approximately 0.02. This implies that the evidence is uncommon and therefore significant. But what is the probability of finding the evidence given that the man is innocent? Since we can expect all of the men who work in the mine to have the evidence on them, we can estimate this using the ratio 199/200; approximately 0.995. This gives a very different impression since such evidence is extremely common on the mineworkers. These probabilities illustrate the prosecutor's fallacy; in fact, the probability of the mineral traces given that the man works in the mine indicate he is much more likely to be innocent than guilty. The use of Bayesian reasoning for evaluation of evidence is not universally accepted and has presented some difficulties in court due to its complexity. However, most statisticians and many forensic scientists consider it to be the most effective method.

DNA databases

The world's first DNA database was created in England and Wales in 1995. There are now over sixty million DNA profiles stored in databases in over sixty states around the world. The largest database is in China (over forty-four million profiles) followed by the USA (over seventeen million profiles). The UK DNA database contains around six million profiles, the highest proportion (over 8 per cent) of any population in the world. Ninety per cent of these profiles are from known individuals and the remainder are from crime scene stains. In the UK, the chance of obtaining a match between a new profile being placed on the database and a crime stain already present is over 60 per cent, although fewer than 1 per cent of crimes are detected by DNA. The true impact of DNA databases on criminal justice is still not well understood.

The rationale for most databases follows the same general principles: most crimes are committed by a minority of individuals; many of these individuals re-offend; most criminals are involved in a range of crimes; many individuals involved in serious crime are also involved in minor crime. Therefore retaining DNA (and fingerprints) from convicted persons means that offenders who already have convictions can be identified and arrested more quickly.

There is no standard model for a DNA database in terms of what samples can be taken and how long they can be kept. A few countries sample the entire population, most other countries take samples from convicted individuals, arrested individuals, volunteers, or a combination of all three. In some countries, DNA profiles are stored only for certain serious offences. In other countries, samples are stored but are eventually destroyed. In federal states such as the USA and Australia the rules for sampling and storage vary between states.

DNA profiling provides a powerful tool for the investigation of crime because it can be used to analyse the blood and body fluids that are transferred in a wide range of crimes. The method of analysis uses multiple tests that can be carried out quickly and economically on extremely small amounts. The analysis is highly discriminating and provides very strong evidence. This means that offenders can be rapidly identified if their profiles are stored on a database, and intelligence-led screens (mass screens) can be used to eliminate large numbers of individuals, many of whom may be volunteers. Furthermore, an offender who is not on the database but who has a relative on it can (in serious cases only) be identified indirectly by 'familial searching' because they will have a similar DNA profile.

Other methods of DNA analysis

Until now we have been discussing nuclear or somatic DNA, the DNA that is found in most cells. There are a number of other types of DNA analysis that can be used for forensic purposes including Y-STR analysis and mtDNA analysis. Y-STRs are found on the Y chromosome so are only found in males and are passed down the male line. All male children with the same father will have the same Y-STRs. Mitochondria are organelles found in the cytoplasm of most cells and are passed through the female line. All children from the same mother will have the same mtDNA. The nature of the DNA in both cases is different from somatic DNA and the methods of analysis and interpretation are also different. Y-STR analysis can be particularly valuable in sexual offences where it can both identify the presence of male DNA and be used to compare this with a possible offender. MtDNA can be used to analyse hair shafts and is useful in dealing with highly degraded DNA that might be encountered in ancient remains or mass disasters. There are no databases for Y-STR or mtDNA in the sense of the databases used for somatic DNA and the significance of the evidence obtained is much lower.

The potential to predict the physical characteristics of an individual from DNA analysis has been long imagined and long promised. In recent years there have been some developments in this area. Eye colour, skin colour, and hair colour predictions can be made that are around 85 per cent accurate. Hair colour is less useful than the others because it changes over time and can be altered by common treatments or be removed. The accuracy and reliability of these techniques is still too low for them to be used systematically in investigations but it is likely that current methods will be improved.

Finally, the future of DNA analysis lies in a method known as next generation sequencing (NGS) or massive parallel sequencing (MPS) depending on whose terminology is used. As the names suggest these are DNA technologies that can analyse millions to billions of DNA sequences. Many advantages are likely to come from NGS including the ability to analyse smaller samples and better differentiation of samples, as well as information about the physical appearance and the biogeographic ancestry of the sample donor.

Chapter 6
Prints and marks: more ways to identify people and things

Marks (or impressions) are caused by a pattern from one item being transferred to another. This could be a shoe mark, a finger mark, or, less obviously, the pattern of striations on a plastic bag made by a tool in the manufacturing process. Firing pins in guns (see Figure 11), as well as saws, tyres and screwdrivers, can all leave marks that can be used to identify the general type of object that made them (a shoe, a tyre) and sometimes the specific object. This chapter uses fingerprints and shoe marks to illustrate the general characteristics of marks evidence, the principles involved in their examination, and how the evidence is evaluated.

Fingerprints and shoe marks are the most important and frequently encountered evidence of this type. With most of these examiners believe identification of an object (or an individual by fingerprints) can be done unequivocally, that is, with complete certainty. We have everyday experience of marks and have ourselves on occasions made such judgements: who muddied the kitchen floor—a small boy (a shoe mark) or a small dog (a paw mark)? Understanding the application of marks to the investigation of crime is an extension of this everyday experience.

Marks can be visible (patent) or invisible (latent) and require specialist optical, physical, or chemical techniques to visualize them. They can be made in a variety of substances: mud, blood,

11. Striations on bullet casing. This image illustrates a recovered cartridge and test-fired cartridge under a comparison microscope showing matching striations on both cartridges indicating the bullets have been fired by the same weapon.

dust, sweat—referred to as 'negative' marks—or by transferring a material to another surface—'positive' marks. A shoe stepping into a pool of blood can leave a negative mark in the blood followed by positive marks on the floor walked upon.

A characteristic feature of many marks is that one can identify the type of item that made the mark from examination of the mark's general characteristics. The appearance of the mark generally represents the shape of the item, its main features, and their spatial arrangement. Shoe marks, finger marks, and tyre marks are readily identifiable often from a cursory visual examination, though this is not always the case. Marks can also provide further information about the type of item that made them. Not just a shoe but a particular type of shoe (a trainer, say), or a saw with a certain number of teeth per inch, or a screwdriver of a certain blade width. This provides the opportunity to derive inceptive information or intelligence for the investigator in the absence of the item or a suspect. Knowing what the item is allows the police to look out for it. If information from large numbers of marks is compiled as a database, it can be used as intelligence to link crime scenes. Such databases are widely used in fingerprints.

Despite the wide range of objects that make marks, the processes and aim of any comparison are very similar: to determine whether there is a connection or otherwise between the mark and the reference object, and if so to what degree. We have already discussed the nature of identity and how DNA matches are evaluated in probabilistic terms, but this process is not used for marks identifications. Instead, following the gradual accumulation of similarities between the mark and reference item, there comes a point when the examiner decides that it matches this reference item (shoe, tool, finger) and no other. In scientific terms, this is an odd conclusion since it cannot be justified on logical grounds. For such a conclusion to be logical, the examiner would have to have compared the mark with all other reference marks currently in existence. Yet most examiners are prepared to state such a conclusion, and the courts are generally content to receive such conclusions since they much prefer evidence that is clear and easy to understand. We will consider this issue further under fingerprints. The quality of the mark, that is, the amount of information and detail present, is crucial to determining whether it matches and the degree of matching. The comparison process routinely carried out in forensic science laboratories follows a similar general procedure for most marks examinations and addresses the following questions:

- What are the characteristics and features of the mark?
- Can they be observed in the reference item?
- Do the characteristics and features of the mark correspond to the reference item?
- Do any characteristics appear to be different?
- How significant are the matching features?

- Are any differences significant (should the mark be eliminated or are the differences explicable)?
- How significant is the match?

Another important consideration is how to evaluate differences between the mark and reference item. Such differences do not necessarily mean the item should be eliminated. Tools, shoes, and tyres wear as they are used and will continue to wear after they have deposited any marks. This can result in new features (which are not in the mark) due to damage, or loss of pattern features as the mark wears. Any differences must be evaluated carefully by the examiner on the basis of their knowledge and experience.

Fingerprints

'Fingerprint' is a byword for identification and identity. It is widely used in everyday language to refer to any set of characteristics that define an object, activity, or even style. Of the differing types of impressions encountered in forensic work, fingerprints are a particular case since they are biological in origin, not manufactured, and because they directly link to individuals, as does DNA. Fingerprints have been used to identify victims and criminals around the world for over a hundred years, and there are records from over eight million individuals stored on the UK national database (IDENT1). Fingerprints arise from a particular type of skin called friction ridge skin found on the fingers, palms of the hands, and the soles of the feet. This skin has patterns of ridges and furrows which can be transferred in sweat to other items when they are touched, for example when picking up a drinking glass. The origin of these patterns is genetic and they develop in the foetus in the womb. However, they are also subject to non-genetic influence since identical twins have different fingerprints.

The examination of fingerprints is based on the detailed characteristics which form the patterns of ridges and which can be compared. Unless damaged in some way, these skin patterns persist throughout life, providing a powerful biometric which can be used to identify individuals and store records in databases. Fingerprints are routinely used in most countries around the world to check that an individual who is arrested is who they say they are and whether they have come to police attention previously. They are also used as a means of identity in non-criminal situations for security purposes such as building and computer access. Fingerprints are perhaps best known as a means of identifying individuals and linking them to a crime scene or an item, such as a weapon or vehicle, that may inculpate them. Despite this widely known fact and that transfer of fingerprints can be easily prevented by wearing gloves, they are still found at crime scenes around the world in vast numbers, and the examination of fingerprints is one of the most important and valuable areas of forensic practice.

In many countries, fingerprint examination is separate from the rest of forensic science for reasons that are perhaps historic (and rather too lengthy to go into here) but are no longer justifiable. The current physical, methodological, cognitive, and cultural separation of fingerprints from other areas of forensic science serves neither the interests of justice nor the long-term interest of the fingerprint community In a few countries such as Scotland and Finland all specialist forensic services reside in a single organization, an arrangement that is more likely to provide consistent and higher standards of practice.

History

The idea of fingerprints as an identifier has been around for millennia; for example, marks were used historically to identify ownership of clay pots in the ancient world. The modern history of fingerprint examination began around a hundred years ago, and the first case in the UK to use marks from crime scenes was in 1902. In 1900, the UK abandoned Bertillon's anthropometric system as impractical and ineffective, and fingerprints were adopted as the sole means of identification. Many individuals, particularly Francis Galton, the English polymath and cousin of Charles Darwin, were responsible for developing procedures for fingerprint examination and encouraging their use. Although there have been some alterations over the years, the processes developed in the early part of the 20th century essentially remained in use until the development of computerized automatic fingerprint identification systems (AFIS) in the 1980s and live scan technology (digital capture of fingerprints) in the 1990s. Nowadays fingerprints from individuals and marks from crime scenes can be recorded electronically and checked against databases in real time using portable devices.

Features of fingerprints

Until now we have used the terms 'print' and 'mark' interchangeably, but there is an important convention in the use of this terminology. Both terms refer to patterns deposited onto surfaces, but the word 'print' refers to impressions made by the known source. When impressions are taken from an individual as records and to identify the individual, these are referred to as 'fingerprints'. The sets of all ten finger impressions taken for police records are referred to as 'ten-prints' in the UK. Impressions from fingers left on objects are referred to as 'finger marks', or simply 'marks'. This is an important distinction between circumstances where the source of the impression is known and those where it is unknown but can be inferred following examination. In the USA and many other countries marks are called latent prints and fingerprint examiners are often called latent print examiners.

Marks are generally formed from sweat left on the surface of the skin ridges. The deposited residue is composed mainly of water but also contains proteins, amino acids, fatty acids, inorganic salts, cholesterol, and squalene. The amount of residue left by an individual depends on many variables including the condition of the skin and the diet, age, sex, and physical condition of the donor. The surface on which a mark is deposited is also important. Marks left on porous surfaces such as paper may remain for decades because the residue is absorbed. In contrast, marks on a non-porous surface are prone to abrasion and their persistence is significantly influenced by the subsequent handling of the item.

There are three main patterns of ridges: loops, whorls, and arches (see Figure 12), and these can be used to classify prints and marks or rapidly exclude a mark that has a distinctly different pattern. The ridges are not continuous but composed of characteristics known as *minutiae* including bifurcations, ridge endings, and other related phenomena. The ability to characterize a fingerprint and identify a donor is based primarily on the sequence of minutiae in the print and mark. These sequences are extraordinarily discriminating (like DNA) and the amount of

12. **Fingerprint ridge patterns. This shows the three main categories used: loop (right), whorl (left), and arch (top). Non-matching patterns can be used to rapidly eliminate a mark.**

information in a mark is often highly redundant. The same mark can often be identified in a number of different ways and it is not uncommon for different fingerprint experts who have matched a mark to do so using a different sequence of minutiae. For an identification, there must be a significant number of minutiae *in sequence and agreement* and no significant or inexplicable differences. Two of the main minutiae are illustrated in Figure 13(a), together with a comparison of an unknown mark with a reference print in Figure 13(b).

In addition to the pattern of the mark and sequence of minutiae, other features such as the pattern of minute pores on the tops of the ridges can also be used to identify marks.

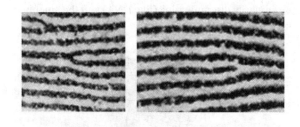

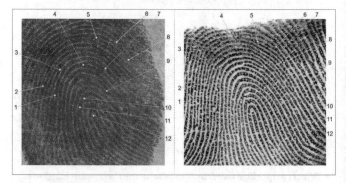

13. (a) Fingerprint minutiae: bifurcation (left) and ridge ending (right). **(b)** Fingerprint comparison of mark (left) and print (right).

Recovery of marks

The oldest and most common method for recovering latent marks is the use of fine powders which are applied to the mark by a brush. Commercial powders are available in differing materials, particle size, shape, and colour which can be used on surfaces of different textures and colours. Powders such as aluminium, the most common one used, tend to adhere to the fatty components of the residue. These work best on non-porous surfaces and less well on others, but they have the advantage of simplicity and ease of application. There are many other techniques for the detection and visualization of latent marks which depend on the type of the surface on which the mark is deposited and components in the residue of the mark. Lasers and ultraviolet light can be used to cause fluorescence of marks which can then be photographed. Marks can also be enhanced by chemicals that react with specific components in the residue. One of the best-known methods uses ninhydrin, a protein stain, to react with amino acids in the mark. This is very effective for porous surfaces and is commonly used to develop marks on paper. A common chemical method for non-porous surfaces uses vaporized cyanoacrylate (superglue) which reacts with the residue, rendering it visible as pale grey marks. These methods are frequently applied in a logical sequence following a well-known publication, the *Fingerprint Source Book* published by the Home Office Centre for Applied Technology in the UK.

Fingerprint comparison

When comparing marks to prints, there is now widespread acceptance amongst fingerprint examiners of a standard methodology that is denoted by the acronym ACE-V: analysis, comparison, evaluation, and verification. Some experts say this method is scientific; it isn't, it's just a logical way to approach a fingerprint examination.

- Analysis. In this stage, a detailed assessment of the quality and level of information in a mark is made. Issues such as the possible substrate and its influence on the mark are considered. The effects of distortion and pressure are also taken into account, which enables the examiner to allow for minute variations (tolerances) between the mark and print.

- Comparison. This is the 'side-by-side' examination to establish correspondences (or lack of them) between the mark and print. The mark should be examined first and the print next, and if the reverse process is used it should be done with great care and specifically recorded in the case notes.

- Evaluation. In light of any correspondences between the print and mark, the examiner makes a judgement: can the mark be eliminated or does it match? If it matches, is the degree of correspondence sufficient to identify an individual? This judgement is an inference and therefore subjective. It is an opinion not a fact.

- Verification. A second experienced and qualified fingerprint expert reviews the comparison and conclusion following the ACE-V protocol. Ideally this is done independently but this may not be practical in small organizations.

Traditionally the outcome of this process is one of three possible conclusions. The first of these is an *identification* (or 'individualization', as it is called in some parts of the world), which means that the mark is attributed to one person to the exclusion of all others. The second possibility is *exclusion*: the person whose prints have been used for comparison could not have made the mark. The third category is *inconclusive* (or insufficient): that is, no judgement can be made about the mark (usually due to poor quality or lack of detail present) for the purposes of a criminal investigation or prosecution. A little reflection on this third category will immediately reveal it as problematic.

Let's consider these outcomes in a little more detail. If there are significant differences between a mark and a print, an individual can be excluded. This is analogous to practices elsewhere in forensic science—exclusion is often a very straightforward business. One critical difference is enough, irrespective of what is being compared (DNA, hairs, fibres, paint fragments). Identification takes place when the examiner considers there has been sufficient accumulation of elements (minutiae, etc.) that lead them to form the view that a mark can be attributed unequivocally to an individual. Marks that fall between these two categories are deemed inconclusive, but this must include a range of marks with different levels of information present. Some of these will contain little or no information: perhaps a pattern and one or two minutiae. Others will contain considerable detail, although not enough for identification, but does this mean they are of no value? In most other areas of forensic science where evidence falls short of complete correspondence but reveals matching features the examiner will comment on the significance of the match. This practice of categorizing non-identifiable evidence as inconclusive is unique to fingerprints, and we will return to this point towards the end of this chapter.

Identification standards

Fingerprint identification standards have been developing over the past fifty years or so, but this has not always been logical nor based on fact. The situation has also been different in different countries around the world, but there are some commonalities. For many years it was generally agreed in the fingerprint world that a specified number of minutiae in sequence and agreement (and no differences) were required in order to identify a mark. This number varied in different countries and even sometimes within one country. Until 2001 in most of the UK (2006 in Scotland), the number was sixteen minutiae—colloquially and inaccurately referred to as 'the sixteen-point standard'. This was not in fact a standard but a numerical threshold or bar of convenience for fingerprint experts. This meant that a mark having sixteen points could be identified but one that had fewer (other than in certain specific circumstances) could not. There was no halfway house—if only fourteen points were present, the mark was not identified. Gradually numeric standards lost credibility in the fingerprint world with the acceptance that there was no logical basis for them. A notable study on this issue was carried out by Ian Evett and Ray Williams in 1988 in which they identified so much variation in the attribution of numbers of minutiae between different experts, it became obvious that obtaining sixteen points had very little to do with 'standards'. Amongst other important findings, they established that the sixteen-point standard was based on false evidence. Evett and Williams were also concerned by the practice by some experts of using the print as a 'guide' to examining the mark. This can lead to confirmation bias, where the examiner, having seen the original print, looks to find (consciously or unconsciously) the same features in the mark. This is a bit like looking at the night sky for a constellation, you are looking for a pattern that you expect to find: there is no pattern there—you are imposing the pattern on a random distribution of stars in the sky. Not only are you likely to see the pattern if you expect it, but you will also have trouble seeing things that do not fit that pattern and may not perceive them. The review was quietly set aside by the Home Office in the UK but was later published in 1995.

In 1997, Marion Ross was murdered in her home in Ayrshire, Scotland. During the course of the crime a biscuit tin containing £1,400 was stolen. The biscuit tin was recovered and a fingermark was found on it that was attributed to a man called David Asbury. At the time, Shirley McKie was a police officer with Strathclyde Police. In the course of the murder investigation a fingermark found inside the murder scene was attributed to McKie. At the murder trial McKie denied having been inside the house. Asbury was convicted and when the case was concluded McKie was charged with perjury. The only evidence against McKie was the fingermark. At her trial for perjury in 1999 the jury did not believe the fingerprint experts and acquitted McKie after twenty minutes' deliberation. In August 2002, it was accepted by the appeal court in Scotland that the fingerprint evidence against Asbury was unreliable and his conviction was quashed.

The 'Scottish case', as it was often referred to by fingerprint experts seeking to distance themselves from the issues it raised, caused an international scandal in the world of fingerprints and beyond. An image of the crime scene mark was published in national newspapers and on the internet, and the fingerprint world was divided about whether the mark matched McKie or not. The debate was polarized and at times venomous. On other occasions it was characterized by posturing and nonsense. Much of the venom and nonsense came from a sect of fingerprint experts from around the world who believed their methodologies were infallible and that mistakes of any kind were impossible. The scandal led to a Scottish Parliamentary Inquiry in 2006 (which I advised) and a Public Inquiry in 2009. The McKie family sued the Scottish Government, who made an out of court settlement of £750,000 (around US$1 million). The public inquiry put an end to the debate in legal terms: the fingermark was not a match with Shirley McKie.

In 2004, an equally dramatic scandal took place in the United States following the train bombings in Madrid. The Spanish National Police circulated fingermarks from the bombing to police organizations around the world. The FBI identified Brandon Mayfield as the source of one of these marks, and he was arrested and imprisoned. The Spanish Police on the other hand attributed the same mark to a man called Daoud. The FBI travelled to Spain to re-examine the original mark and decided that it contained insufficient detail to be identified. Sometime later the FBI and the Spanish police met again to resolve the situation. The FBI issued a second report attributing the fingermark to Daoud and stating that the identification of Mayfield was an error. In 2006, the US government apologized to Mayfield and settled a US$2 million lawsuit.

Both of these cases had enormous ramifications for fingerprint evidence. They exposed inadequate standards, poor training, dysfunctional systems, professional arrogance, dishonesty, and bias of various kinds. The issues continue to resonate in the forensic world today. Much research has been done and the debate is rather more civilized today, but it will probably take a generation to fully understand the issues and resolve them. Fingerprints are a reliable means of identification but there are important issues about procedures, standards, and the training of experts that still need to be addressed. The process of moving from an arcane practice, taken for granted for over a century, to a more transparent, rational one requiring a complete overhaul of the culture of fingerprint experts will be difficult and will take a long time.

Shoe marks

Footwear marks are used in a wide variety of investigations. They can indicate the position of individuals in a scene and their movements, which may be important to the investigation or prosecution of a case. For example, a shoe mark found near a window may be a good indication that this was the point of entry (or exit) in a burglary. Shoe marks can be recovered in very similar ways to fingerprints. The most common method used is photography, which must include a scale so that the mark can be reproduced for life-size comparison. Latent marks can also be visualized using the same optical, chemical, and physical enhancement processes as were mentioned for fingerprints. There are a number of important features used in examination of shoe marks: the tread pattern, that is, the arrangement of the various individual elements that make up the sole (lines, circles, squares, logos, etc.); the tread pattern dimensions—the sizes of individual elements and overall size of the pattern; manufacturing features such as mould marks, bubbles, and knife marks from trimming; progressive wear, which results in gradual loss of detail in the pattern as the shoe is worn; and specific damage—individual and characteristic elements of damage such as cuts caused by wear or defects from the manufacturing process.

All of these can be used individually or in combination to examine shoe marks, and this usually involves producing a test impression of the sole. When comparing an unknown mark and known shoe print, the larger the area of the tread represented and the better the definition, the more information there is available to determine an association or exclusion. Non-matching features must be considered in this process. Differences that do not have a reasonable explanation should result in the examiner excluding the footwear from having made the mark. A difference in pattern would exclude the shoe immediately and could take place very quickly if the patterns are noticeably different.

In addition to the tread pattern, there are other aspects of the way a mark was made that affect its appearance. For example, the amount of pressure on the tread and the degree of movement involved in deposition can result in distortion of the pattern (as in fingerprints). Unstable surfaces such as soil or sand can also lower the mark quality.

In 2005, a few days after Christmas, a young child was abducted from her home in the north-east of England. She was later found a few streets away, naked and bleeding, and had been sexually assaulted. A partial DNA profile was obtained from the body of the child but this did not lead to the identification of the offender. A partial shoe mark was found at the crime scene and from this the type and size of shoe was identified. Investigators established that around sixty pairs of these shoes had been sold in the surrounding area and they set about tracing the owners of the shoes. In January the following year, investigators went to the home of a local man, Peter Voisey. The first thing the detectives noticed when Voisey answered his door was that he was wearing the type of shoes they were looking for. After further inquiries Voisey was arrested, and his shoes and a DNA sample taken from him. The partial DNA profile was found to match Voisey and the shoe mark from the scene matched his shoes. He was later tried and convicted of kidnap, rape, and indecent assault.

We have considered marks and impression evidence, with particular focus on shoe marks and fingerprints, and their important role in the investigation of crime. In general terms, marks and impression evidence are at something of a watershed due to criticism of some of the methodologies used and the dangers these may present. It is likely that we will continue to see significant changes in procedures in this area which will require large-scale alterations to working practices and the training of those involved. This is necessary for them to keep pace with developments in other areas of forensic science and to maintain their essential contribution to the investigation and prosecution of crime.

Chapter 7
Trace evidence

In many ways, the concept of trace evidence epitomizes forensic science. The idea that tiny fragments of materials, invisible to the naked eye and therefore unknown to those involved, can be used to investigate crime is a powerful one which catches the imagination as well as being of practical value. Fibres, hairs, paint, glass, and explosives traces are examined by forensic scientists in a wide range of crimes from burglary to terrorism. The distinctive characteristics of trace evidence are its microscopic size or minute amount (so, its 'invisibility'), its ability to transfer readily from one item to another, and that it is subsequently lost from the item following that transfer. Many of the issues we will explore and the difficulties that arise in the examination, analysis, and interpretation of trace evidence are consequences of these characteristics. The minute amounts involved require specialist techniques to recover and analyse the evidence, as well as stringent precautions to prevent contamination at scenes and in the laboratory. This chapter describes what most forensic scientists would refer to as 'contact trace evidence', and we will consider the principles that underlie trace evidence examination, some of the scientific techniques used, how the significance of the evidence is assessed, and the importance of trace evidence in police investigations.

Trace evidence can come from a bewildering range of sources: natural and synthetic. We will confine ourselves to fibres and paint as examples that demonstrate the many characteristics typical of trace evidence. There is no agreed size at which materials become categorized as trace evidence. Larger fragments can often be seen by the naked eye, for example single fibres and some paint and glass particles, although we could not search for such particles effectively using the unaided eye. The reasons why these particles are so small differs depending on the evidence type. For fibres, it may be due to fragmentation of synthetic fibres (which can be very long) or the short length of individual natural fibres such as wool or cotton. Glass is often shattered into fragments during the commission of the crime. The next important characteristic of trace evidence is that it is easily and often quickly lost, almost as easily as it is transferred. How long the material stays in place is usually referred to as its 'persistence'. The twin concepts of transfer and persistence are critical to the understanding of trace evidence, as we saw in Chapter 1.

Fibres

Textiles are all around us, in our homes, cars, and workplaces, in the form of clothing, upholstery, and fabrics of all kinds. Most fabrics are mass produced from natural or synthetic fibres. We know from our everyday experience that fibres readily transfer from one item to another—light fibres show up easily on dark clothing. In the investigation of crime, fibres can be used to associate individuals with other individuals or crime scenes, vehicles, or items associated with a crime. This would include, for example, the potential to connect an individual to a particular seat in a vehicle, with a balaclava which was used in an armed robbery, or with the clothing of a victim who had been physically attacked. Fibres can also be recovered from weapons such as knives or guns, and from vehicles in 'hit and run' cases. We need to make an important distinction between the evidence (the fibres) found and the inferences which may be drawn from them. Strictly speaking, we are not linking individuals or scenes but clothing, items, or fabrics; and the significance of any finding will depend on the detailed circumstances of the case.

Recovery and examination of fibres is a laborious and painstaking process that rarely yields conclusive evidence, and can slow down the examination of other types of evidence which are potentially more fruitful. In a homicide where blood has been shed, any blood found is likely to yield better evidence as it can be attributed with great confidence to its source by DNA profiling. In such a case, fibres may be recovered (which in itself takes a great deal of time) but are unlikely to be examined. In cases where it is accepted that the parties involved have been in contact, or where they have a prior association which could explain the presence of fibres found, a fibres examination would not be carried out. This happens in many cases where the individuals involved are related, share the same home or workplace, or were in contact prior to the incident, for example in a pub or club. Generally, one can only comment on fibres evidence when fibres have been found. In rare instances, it may be possible to draw certain inferences from the absence of fibres, but this is difficult due to the number of imponderable factors involved. Prior to an examination taking place, a lot of information is needed by the scientist to assess the likelihood of finding fibres and their potential significance to an investigation. In doing so, the scientist will pose the following question: how likely is it that fibres have been transferred that are likely to be recovered and could provide evidence of significance? Strictly speaking, this question can only be answered by carrying out the work, but in most cases reasonable predictions of the outcome can be made on the basis of knowledge, experience, and the details of the case. Table 5 sets out the factors that need to be considered in this process.

Once the items have been taped, the tapings are searched for a 'target fibre'. In a typical clothing examination, this will be a single fibre type (clothing often contains more than one fibre type) from one item that has good prospects of being found if present and of

Table 5. Determining the potential value of a fibres examination.

Is the integrity of the items sound?	Are there any issues of contamination? Have the items been recovered, packaged, and sealed appropriately?
Does the donor item shed fibres?	Fleecy items shed fibres more readily than smooth items. Natural fibres tend to shed more easily than synthetic fibres.
Will the recipient item retain fibres?	Very smooth surfaces will lose fibres more quickly than rough or fleecy surfaces.
Has there been sufficient contact to transfer fibres?	The longer the contact, the bigger the area, and the higher the pressure involved, the more likely it is that transfer will have taken place.
Was the recipient item recovered in time to minimize loss of any transferred fibres?	Most fibres are lost rapidly after transfer, especially if this is to the clothing of someone who is moving. Fibres on stationary items, e.g. car seats, will remain in place for much longer.
Can the fibres be recovered?	The fibres need to be sufficiently coloured to be seen under a low-power microscope and contrast sufficiently with the donor item. It may be impossible to find blue fibres from one garment on another blue garment even if they are there.
Are the fibres likely to provide significant evidence?	Some fibres are so common in the environment that they are likely to be found on most items and therefore mean very little. Black cotton and cotton from blue jeans are examples of this.

potential evidential significance. This usually means a fibre of a recognizable colour that can be separated from the background. The tapings are then systematically examined for fibres similar to the target, and any found are removed and mounted individually on microscope slides. This can take many hours and can be like looking for the proverbial needle in a haystack. Each fibre is then compared under a high-power comparison microscope. This microscope (see Figure 14) allows the examination of the

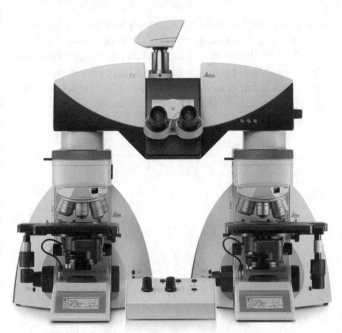

14. **Comparison microscope. This allows the examination of the recovered fibre and control sample simultaneously under the same lighting conditions.**

recovered fibre and control sample simultaneously under the same lighting conditions.

Many of the fibres recovered will not match and will be discarded as this first stage is a fairly crude process. The features examined during the comparison process include colour, fibre type, and the cross-sectional shape of the fibre. Fibres that match move on to the next stage for detailed analysis, which includes measurement and comparison of the colour and analysis of the polymers in synthetic fibres. Most natural fibres can be identified by microscopy alone. The colour of the fibre is analysed and compared by microspectrophotometry. A microspectrophotometer is a specialist microscope with a spectrophotometer attached. This measures the colour spectrum of the fibre (illustrated in Figure 15) and allows more objective comparison than is possible using normal high-power microscopy. The process is very discriminating, but in many laboratories further analysis is carried out on the dyes in individual fibres, which may be only a few

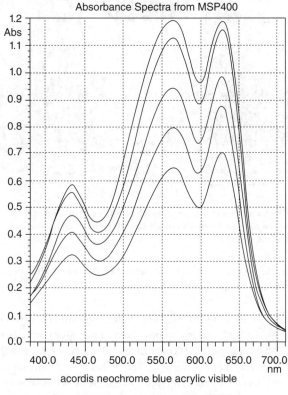

Absorbance Spectra from MSP800.

15. Colour spectra of blue acrylic fibres. Examination of such spectra allows the matching or elimination of individual recovered fibres when compared to a control sample from a garment.

millimetres long. Thin-layer chromatography (TLC) is a simple chromatographic technique that can separate dyes into their individual colour components. Over 7,000 different dyes are produced worldwide and these are used in many combinations. TLC can often discriminate between fibres that are indistinguishable in the other tests, and sometimes associate the fibres with an individual dye batch.

Wool, cotton, and many vegetable fibres can be readily identified by microscopy, but synthetic fibres require chemical analysis to confirm their type. The most common method used in forensic science laboratories is Fourier Transform Infrared Spectroscopy (FTIR). Infrared spectroscopy can be used to identify substances on the basis of their molecular vibrations. Different molecular groups absorb infrared radiation at specific wavelengths, resulting in a spectrum that can be used to identify the polymer type present. In FTIR, a mathematical process (Fourier transformation) is used which allows faster collection and analysis of the data. From this analysis, the scientist can identify the type of fibre and in many cases the presence of other polymers which allow sub-typing of the fibre.

The above processes have to take place for every suitable item involved and can result in the recovery and examination of many thousands of fibres, and take many weeks. The final stage is the interpretation of the evidence. In addition to the detailed findings and specific context of the case, the main factors considered here are set out in Table 6.

Between 30 October and 10 December 2006, five women were murdered near Ipswich in Suffolk. All of the women were prostitutes and all were found naked. The bodies of two of the women (Tania Nicol and Gemma Adams) were found in a brook. The bodies of Anneli Alderton, Annette Nichols, and Paula Clennell were found in woodland. All of the women had been asphyxiated but there was no evidence that they had been sexually assaulted.

Table 6. Evaluating the significance of fibres evidence: factors that are considered in determining the significance of recovered matching fibres.

Numbers of fibres	The more matching fibres found, the more confident one can be of direct contact. Very small numbers of fibres may be due to indirect contact from an indistinguishable source.
Types and proportions of fibres found	The more different types of fibres found and the closer they match the proportions of fibres shed by an item, the more confident one can be that they derive from a common source.
Colour and dye type	Different chemical classes of dye are used in different fibre types. The more distinctive the combination of colour and dyes, the more probative is the match.
Quality of analysis	Some tests are more discriminating than others. A highly discriminating test will increase the significance of matching fibres and the reverse for a poorly discriminating test.
Commonness of fibres	One might anticipate finding a common fibre by chance and unrelated to the particular case. The more unusual the fibre, the more confident one can be that it is due to a true transfer.
Levels of transfer	Fibres being transferred from one item to another is referred to as a 'one-way transfer'. If fibres from the other item are also transferred, this is referred to as a 'two-way transfer'. Two-way transfer considerably increases the significance of the evidence.

Forensic scientists found a DNA profile from an unknown person that linked the three bodies found in the woodland. On 18 December, a man who fitted the predicted psychological profile of the killer and who had associations with the victims was arrested but his DNA profile did not match that found on the bodies. Shortly afterwards a DNA database match linked the DNA profile to Steve Wright, a forklift truck driver who had recently moved to the 'red light' area of Ipswich. Wright was interviewed by police but made no comment in response to their questions.

An extensive forensic examination of Wright's home and belongings commenced during which DNA profiles matching Clennell and Nichols were found on one of his jackets. Wright was now directly connected with three of the murders but was he also connected with the other two and was there any independent evidence that all of the murders were linked? One way of testing whether the cases were linked was fibre transfer. The bodies of all of the victims had been taped so any fibres present had been recovered. Washings from the hair of the two bodies found in the brook were also made at the post mortem examination. But how could a fibres examination be done in the absence of the victims' clothing (which was never found)? A team of forensic scientists led by Ray Palmer of the Forensic Science Service embarked on an unusual examination. They searched the tapings and categorized fibres from all of the bodies into groups. They established eight groups of fibres that they thought were of particular interest because they were less common. The team cross-searched fibres from each of the bodies to see if any of the groups matched. Searching a taping is a bit like trying to find a matchstick on a football field. In a mammoth exercise, the team searched 1,400 tapings. Items from Wright's home and his car had also been seized, and these were also examined for fibres and other evidence.

The fibres examination yielded the following results:

- thirty-three fibres of eight different types linked Alderton to Wright's home, car, and clothing;
- sixty fibres of six different fibre types linked Nicholls to Wright's car and clothing;
- forty-eight fibres of six different types linked Clennell to Wright's home, car, and clothing;
- twenty-two fibres of five different types linked Nicol to Wright's clothing, home, and car;
- fourteen fibres of two types linked Adams to Wright's clothing, home, and car;

In court, Palmer said the chances of these fibres coming from someone other than Wright or his home environment were 'infinitesimally small'.

In the 1990s, I led a team that carried out a fibres examination of similar scale and scope in one of the UK's largest homicide investigations. Robert Black was arrested in the Scottish borders attempting to abduct a child and was believed to be connected to the deaths of three other children over a period of twelve years. The children had been abducted and their bodies deposited hundreds of miles from where they went missing. Some of the children's clothing was missing and there was no information about what Black had been wearing or even if he still possessed the items that he might have worn at the time of the deaths. We categorized the fibres from the bodies and placed them in a database to identify potential fibres for comparison in a process similar to that carried out by Palmer's team. In this instance no fibres were found. Black was convicted of killing the three children in 1995 on the basis of circumstantial evidence and his distinctive *modus operandus*. In 2011, Black was tried and convicted of the murder of a fourth child in Northern Ireland. He died in prison in 2016 as the UK's most prolific serial killer of children.

Paint

Paint is a complex material with a wide range of potential components but typically includes a coloured pigment suspended in a solvent with other chemical additives. The solvent keeps the paint as a liquid prior to application and the pigment imparts colour. Additives may include chemicals that support the particular method of application, such as spraying, but these evaporate together with the solvent following application. A chemical in the paint known as a binder holds the paint together, forming a hard coating on the surface when dry. Pigments, binders, and other additives derive from a wide range of sources—natural, synthetic, organic, or inorganic—and therefore result in enormous variation in types and colours of paint. In forensic science, two main classes of paint are encountered: those used for decorative purposes in domestic or commercial premises (architectural paint); and those used for vehicles. Decorative paints are typically encountered in burglaries, and motor vehicle paint is most frequently encountered in 'hit and run' incidents or vehicle crashes. These two types of paint are very different in their composition, and this is reflected in the different methods of analysis and in the interpretation of the evidence involved.

If a burglar uses a tool such as a screwdriver or jemmy to force open a painted window or door, the tool will leave marks on the surface and it is likely that paint will be transferred to the tool. The amount of paint transferred will depend on a range of factors including the force used, the type of surface (metal or wood), and the condition and type of paint involved. Since doors and windows are repainted regularly, there is often more than one layer of paint present. There may also have been more than one attempt to force entry in areas where the paint was a different colour or was in a different condition. It is important that the control sample of the paint from the scene is representative of all of the types of paint present and includes all colours and layers. A summary of the steps involved in the examination of a typical paint case is given in Table 7.

In evaluating the significance of any matching paint, the scientist will take a similar approach to that used with fibres evidence, but the details will be different. In brief, the closer the match and the more uncommon the paint, the stronger will be the value of the evidence. This judgement will take into account the range and types of paint present; the number, colour, and sequence of matching layers; and the significance of any other analyses used in the examination. Finally, the specific circumstances of the case must be considered before a final determination of significance is made.

Table 7. Paint examination in a burglary case.

Control sample	Inspect control sample to observe colour and condition of paint without removing from packaging to prevent contamination.
Recovered item	Examine visually and under low-power microscope and individually remove any particles of paint that resemble the control sample.
Comparison	Examine recovered fragments with the control sample using high-power comparison microscopy in white, UV, and polarized light. This takes into account the colours, thickness, and sequence of layers present, and the type of pigment if granular.
Analysis	A wide range of analytical techniques can be used to examine the various components of the paint, including MSP (colour), FTIR (binders, pigments, additives), and X-ray spectroscopy (individual elements such as metals).

In Chapter 4, I explained how DNA evidence connected Robert Napper to the murder of Rachel Nickell. This was not the only potential forensic link to Napper. More than sixty tiny fragments of red paint were found in hair combings from Rachel Nickell's 2-year-old son who was with her when she was killed. Napper owned a red painted toolbox. The paint fragments from the hair and the paint from the toolbox were microscopically and chemically similar but this was not enough to provide a definitive match. A more sophisticated test (pyrolysis gas chromatography—mass spectrometry) would be required to achieve this but the fragments were too small for this test. The forensic scientist concluded that a connection between the paint fragments and the tool box could not be ruled out but he was unable to evaluate the likelihood of this. This illustrates the limitations of trace evidence both in terms of the ability to analyse traces as well as interpretation of findings.

Chapter 8
Drugs and toxicology

A drug is a chemical substance that alters the physiological state of a living organism. Drugs in the treatment of medical conditions have a wide range of effects such as analgesia (pain relief) or anaesthesia. In addition to their medical uses, many drugs are taken for pleasure. Caffeine is the most widely used psychoactive substance—a drug that acts primarily on the central nervous system (CNS). Many drugs are also used illicitly. These can be illegal substances in themselves (cannabis, heroin) or pharmaceutical products that are obtained or used illegally. Illicit drug use varies greatly from country to country. In Scotland, benzodiazepines, drugs commonly prescribed to treat anxiety and insomnia, are commonly misused. Abuse of fentanyl, a narcotic analgesic eighty times more potent than morphine, is a problem of epidemic proportions in the USA. Our favourite drug by a very large margin—alcohol—is a source of pleasure but is also intimately connected with a wide range of social harms and crimes from domestic abuse to rape.

The effect of a drug depends on a number of factors including how it enters the body, how much of the active agent reaches the 'target' organ, and an individual's tolerance of the substance. Many pharmaceutical products and illicit drugs are taken by mouth, some are injected, others are inhaled. Some illicit drugs such as cannabis or heroin can be smoked. The route into the body can determine how much and how quickly a drug reaches its maximum level. Cannabis when ingested takes around two hours to reach its peak concentration in the blood in comparison to about thirty seconds when it is smoked. The dose of a drug required for it to have an effect, medicinal or recreational, is determined by the concentration of the substance in the body tissue involved. If the dose is too low the drug may have no effect; it is impossible to get drunk on low alcohol (0.5 per cent ABV) beer. If the dose is too high the drug may cause adverse effects or be poisonous. Almost any substance can result in harm if a high enough dose is taken. Common substances like table salt and water if taken in large enough amounts or too quickly can be hazardous. Even when the dose is controlled, many drugs will have side effects that can be difficult to predict.

Controlled drugs

In most countries, production, supply, or possession of certain substances (and chemicals associated with their manufacture) is illegal. The list of substances is lengthy and differs from country to country. The law in relation to these substances also varies from country to country and sometimes within the same country. Nevertheless, there are many substances that are commonly restricted around the world, notably cannabis, heroin, and amphetamine. There is also an international list of controlled substances upon which many national controlled lists are based. The common rationale for deeming substances to be illegal is the social harm associated with their misuse. Such judgements are complex and involve social, political, legal (and sometimes religious) dimensions as well as scientific and medical ones. Drugs that are considered to have potential for misuse, that are associated with addiction or dependency, or have no currently accepted medical use are often controlled.

In the UK the Misuse of Drugs Act 1971 (MDA) sets out specific restrictions on drugs and the Misuse of Drugs Regulations 2001

(MDR) sets out what is allowable, that is, what *can* be done with drugs. The MDA introduces the concept of a 'controlled drug'—a substance that, due to its harmful properties, ought not to be freely available to the general public. The MDR specifies what can be done with controlled substances, considering their value as medicines as opposed to their potential for misuse. MDR controls the manufacture, prescription, and record-keeping of controlled substances. The MDA differentiates between possession of a controlled drug for personal use, possession with intent to supply (other persons), and production of controlled drugs, with the legal sanctions becoming increasingly severe. Possession requires only minute amounts and is a strict liability offence: it needs no proof of *mens rea*. In addition to specifying which substances are controlled, the MDA also classifies substances on the basis of their perceived harm. Class A drugs are considered to be most harmful and include (for example) crack cocaine, cocaine, diacetylmorphine (heroin), LSD, methadone, methamphetamine (crystal meth), and morphine. Class B drugs include amphetamines, barbiturates, cannabis, codeine, and ketamine. Examples of Class C drugs include benzodiazepines (e.g. diazepam), anabolic steroids, and gamma-hydroxybutyrate (GHB). Assessments of harm are complex judgements made by a committee of experts which advises the UK government and are reviewed from time to time. Nevertheless, some of these assessments remain controversial and many people believe there is little connection between drugs policy (and therefore, ultimately, law) and evidence or rationality.

A recent addition to drugs legislation in the UK is the Psychoactive Substances Act (2016). The purpose of this legislation is to control a range of substances now referred to as new psychoactive substances (NPS), so called 'legal highs'. These substances are chemically diverse but share a common purpose, to simulate the effects of other substances that are illegal. Synthetic cannabinoids such as 'spice' mimic the effect of the major active agent of cannabis, tetrahydrocannabinol (THC). Mephedrone, a synthetic cathinone, is one of many new stimulant drugs that have similar effects to substances like amphetamine and ecstasy. Synthetic cathinones are related to the psychoactive principles in khat (also qat or chat), from the leaves of the plant *Catha edulis*. Other NPS include 'downers', tranquillizer type drugs such as benzodiazepines and hallucinogenic agents. Prior to the legislation these substances were widely available online and from 'head' shops. The main aim of the legislation was to end the trade in 'legal highs'. There is evidence that the legislation has been effective in this respect but it has given forensic chemists an ongoing difficulty. To identify a substance there must be an accepted chemical standard to compare it with. However the chemical nature and diversity of NPS allows them to be constantly modified by illegal laboratories faster than the official laboratories can produce identification standards. This is analogous to the problems in digital forensics due to the rate of technological development in that domain.

Cannabis

The most common illicit drug used in the UK and many other countries is cannabis. The cannabis plant *Cannabis sativa* has been used by humans for thousands of years not only as the source of an intoxicating substance but also as the source of hemp fibres which are used to make ropes and cords. Cannabis is usually encountered in one of three forms: herbal material (marijuana, grass), resin (hash, hashish), and skunk, a particular form of herbal cannabis which we will consider below. The plant grows in a wide variety of environments but requires high temperatures to provide good yields of the drug. Cannabis is often smoked but can also be ingested. THC, the main active ingredient in cannabis, is classed as a mild hallucinogen. Cannabis is illegal in most countries around the world but in many countries the law is not enforced. More recently a number of countries (including several US states) have legalized or decriminalized cannabis use. The physiological consequences of chronic use of cannabis are a matter of dispute although it can lead to dependency. A recent and lengthy report by the USA National Academies concluded that there is little scientific knowledge about the long-term effects of cannabis use.

The amount of THC available depends on the quality of the plants and how they are prepared. Herbal cannabis has the lowest amount of THC and skunk usually has the highest. Cannabis plants, particularly the flowers, contain a resin that can be compacted into hard blocks (hashish) which have a distinctive appearance and smell. Cannabis resin is readily identifiable in most cases from a visual examination, which can be confirmed either by the presence of microscopic hairs (trichomes, which are diagnostic) or chemical analysis to establish the presence of THC. Herbal cannabis consists of dried fragments of plant leaves, flowers, and occasionally seeds. Since it can resemble dried herbs, herbal cannabis cannot be readily identified visually but it can be identified by microscopic examination and chemical analysis. THC can be easily extracted from the flowers and concentrated in a sticky substance known as 'hash oil'. The oil can be smoked, vaped, or ingested. The most commonly encountered form of herbal cannabis in the UK is referred to as 'skunk' because of its characteristic odour. Skunk is a form of sinsemilla, an unusually potent variety of cannabis, which consists of the flowering tops of unfertilized plants that have been grown intensively indoors. All forms of cannabis are Class B drugs in the UK, following reclassification (from class C) in January 2009. Cannabis is a Schedule 1 drug, meaning that it is illegal to produce, possess, and supply it without a Home Office licence. Such licences are only granted for research purposes. While possession of seeds is not illegal (they can be found in birdseed), the cultivation of plants is. Allowing premises to be used for the consumption of cannabis is also an offence. Possession of cannabis is still an arrestable offence, though most people over the age of 18 will likely get a 'cannabis warning' for their first offence.

Heroin

Heroin (diacetylmorphine), morphine, and codeine are opiates that derive from the opium poppy *(Papaver somniferum)*. Heroin is the fanciful name given to diacetylmorphine by its inventors to market it as a safer (non-addictive) version of morphine. Heroin is commonly a white to pale brown powder which is manufactured from the sap of the poppy. It is usually cut with other materials and the purity of the active ingredient varies, although in recent years the purity of most street drugs has risen. Most of the world's heroin comes from Afghanistan. Heroin is usually smoked ('chasing the dragon') or injected, with the latter bringing risk of hepatitis infection and HIV. Opiates depress brain function, and their main medicinal purpose is sedation and pain relief, but they also produce a feeling of calmness and well-being. Opiates are highly addictive, the main rationale for their control. Chronic use of heroin invariably results in poor health, with associated risks of disease, destruction of normal social and family life, and often imprisonment. Diacetylmorphine is a Class A, Schedule 2 drug that can only be legally produced, supplied, and possessed under Home Office licence.

Toxicology

The work of a forensic toxicologist involves the analysis of body fluids and tissues to determine the presence or absence of drugs in the living or the dead. Where the case involves a death, one of the common questions is whether a drug may have caused or had a role in the death. Drug related death is the third most common preventable cause of death of 15–49-year-olds in the UK. The vast majority of these deaths are connected with opioids, substances that produce morphine-like effects. Around half of these deaths involve heroin.

With living persons, the main question to be addressed is whether any drug present may have influenced behaviour or could help us to understand the events that surround the crime. This also includes individuals who have been prescribed regular medication. Someone who has been prescribed an antipsychotic drug, for a condition such as schizophrenia, is likely to experience the recurrence of psychotic episodes if they are not medicated. This may in part explain why they have become the victim or perpetrator of a crime.

Alcohol, more specifically ethyl alcohol or ethanol, is probably the most extensively used recreational drug in the world. It has wide cultural acceptance and close associations with social events and rituals, including religious practices. Alcohol is also associated with much social harm and criminality, to the extent that if it were invented today, it would most likely be a restricted substance. Pharmacologically, alcohol is a CNS depressant. In low doses it promotes feelings of well-being, and can increase self-confidence and sociability. Larger doses can cause mood swings, impaired judgement, and dulled sensory perception. High doses result in a long list of undesirable effects such as confusion, disorientation, nausea, slurred speech, drowsiness, vomiting, and incontinence. Very high doses, around 400 milligrams (mg) per 100 millilitres of blood (400mg per cent) are usually fatal. One of the first faculties that is compromised by alcohol use is judgement, which is one of the reasons why it leads individuals to be caught up in crime, as victims or perpetrators.

Driving while under the influence of alcohol is widely accepted to be dangerous and most countries have legislation to prevent this. The drink-driving limit under English law and in all US States is 80mg per cent in blood or 35 micrograms (μg) per cent of breath. In Scotland and many Continental countries, the limit is lower, 50mg per cent in blood (22μg per cent of breath). Figure 16 shows the relationship between blood alcohol concentration and the likelihood of being involved in a fatal vehicle crash for individuals of different ages. As the alcohol level rises the relative risk rises exponentially. For an individual over 30 years old with

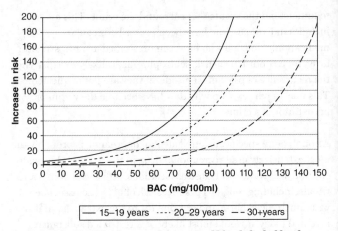

16. **Relative risk of fatal car crash by age and blood alcohol level.**

80mg per cent alcohol in their blood the risk of a crash is sixteen times more likely than without alcohol ingestion. A driver between the ages of 15 and 19 years old with 80mg per cent alcohol in their blood is eighty-seven times more likely to crash than a sober driver of the same age.

Determining if someone is 'over the limit' is straightforward in most cases. The police use an approved hand-held device ('breathalyser') which provides a reliable indication of whether there is alcohol in the driver's breath. If the test is positive the person is arrested and taken to a police station where the alcohol in their breath is measured accurately. Again, this uses a standard instrument, a specially designed and approved infrared spectrometer, following a standard procedure. These results are sufficiently reliable for use in court and do not need expert interpretation. The sanction for drink-driving in the UK is a minimum of twelve months disqualification from driving and a fine. In April 2018 the TV presenter Ant McPartlin was banned

Forensic Science

from driving for twenty months and fined £86,000 (a UK record) for being twice the drink-driving limit. Fines at this level are unusual and tend to be associated with public figures.

There are some circumstances where measuring alcohol concentration is more complicated. For example, say a pedestrian is struck by a car which is then driven away from the scene of the incident. Alcohol is gradually eliminated from the body so the time between the incident and the police finding the alleged driver will have an effect on the alcohol concentration in the body of the driver. It may be that by the time the driver is found his or her alcohol concentration is below the legal limit. But the court is interested in what the concentration of alcohol was at the time of the incident. In these circumstances the prosecution can ask a forensic toxicologist to carry out a 'back calculation' to estimate the alcohol level at the relevant time. The situation is further complicated if the putative driver has been drinking alcohol *after* the incident.

The analysis of blood alcohol in the laboratory uses a technique called 'GC headspace' analysis. This is a form of gas chromatography (GC) that uses a small sample from the air above the sample vial containing the blood (the headspace). The technique separates the chemical components in the sample and compares any alcohol detected with an internal standard (usually propanol). The analysis is comparatively straightforward and is often automated but the interpretation of the results, as in many areas of toxicology, is more complex. Alcohol is eliminated by the body at known rates but there are a number of factors that must also be considered. Knowledge of the detailed timings of the incident and drinking pattern are essential, as well as the weight, height, gender of the donor, and the sample type (blood or urine) taken. Other factors such as the age of the individual involved and whether they have eaten may also be important.

Drug facilitated sexual assault

A variety of substances have been implicated in drug facilitated sexual assault (DFSA), commonly referred to as 'date rape'. Sexual assaults and rape are difficult crimes to investigate because the events are rarely witnessed by others and the evidence is often circumstantial. Even when there is direct evidence of sexual activity, such as a DNA profile, the issue in dispute is often whether the sexual activity was consensual. There is no right to sexual activity, both parties must freely agree, but drugs taken willingly or administered clandestinely can cloud judgement and influence behaviour. Individuals may take risks or act in ways that they otherwise would not. They may become more compliant or less able to physically resist assault. Some drugs can also affect memory. GHB is one of the drugs most frequently implicated by the popular media in date rape. Illicit GHB is commonly sold as a colourless, odourless, bitter tasting liquid. In a drink it can be undetectable to the drinker. GHB is a CNS depressant that causes disinhibition and euphoria at recreational doses but there is only a narrow margin between this and a fatal dose. It is quickly absorbed from the gastrointestinal tract and begins to act in minutes. Its effects can be prolonged by other drugs including alcohol.

A recent study of DFSA in the United States found one or more drugs in 78 per cent of cases. The most common substance detected (31 per cent of cases) was alcohol. Cannabinoids (substances related to the active agent in cannabis) were the second most commonly encountered (29 per cent of cases). The study found many other drugs, often in combination. Alcohol and cannabinoids were found together in 8 per cent of cases. GHB was found in only 6 per cent of the cases but it is a difficult drug to detect for a number of reasons. GHB is a neurotransmitter that is naturally found in the body at low levels. It also has a very short half-life, the time taken for 50 per cent of the drug to be eliminated from the body. The half-life of caffeine is five to six hours. The half-life of GHB is thirty to sixty minutes and some sources quote less than thirty minutes. This means that samples for analysis must be obtained very soon after an incident to have any chance of detecting the substance. Any GHB detected must also be significantly above normal body levels.

Analysis of drugs and interpretation of findings

The forensic toxicologist is faced with a huge number of legal and illegal substances to detect and identify. It is impossible to look for all of them. In some cases, a drug may be suggested from the police investigation or can be inferred from the lifestyle of an individual. One common approach to cases is to use a drug screening method that can indicate the presence of a drug which can then be confirmed by more detailed analysis. A typical screen might test for common prescription drugs such as paracetamol, benzodiazepines, and methadone. Methadone is a heroin substitute used in treatment and rehabilitation of heroin users. Common drugs of abuse in a screen would include many of the drugs already mentioned above. There are many different screening methods but immunological techniques, for example ELISA (enzyme linked immunosorbent assay), are commonly used. ELISA uses an antigen-antibody complex that is specific for an individual drug or drug class. If the relevant drug is present it interferes with the antigen-antibody complex and causes a colour reaction. The process can be automated for the detection of multiple drugs.

Following screening, the most common analytical techniques for identifying and quantifying drugs are various combinations of liquid chromatography and GC with mass spectrometry. In GC the sample is vaporized and passed through a very fine long tube which has a special coating inside. The components in the vaporized sample are separated due to their differing tendencies to stay in the gas or stick to the inside of the tube. Substances are distinguished by how long they take to pass through the tube. The type of gas, the type of coating, tube length, temperature, and so on, all have a bearing on how well components are separated. These parameters can be optimized in advance for each drug or class of drugs.

Samples that have been separated using GC can be analysed using a mass spectrometer (MS). In mass spectrometry, a stream of electrons is used to break up chemical substances and convert them into charged fragments. The fragments are then separated by a magnetic field based on their charge–mass ratio. Individual compounds can be identified by their characteristic mass spectrum. The most basic arrangement for identification for many drugs is the combination of GC and MS (GC-MS). Substances in the sample are separated using GC and identified by MS. There are many refinements to this combination that include different types of chromatography, for example liquid chromatography (LC-MS), or combine multiple MS instruments with different characteristics (quadrupole MS, time of flight MS), but they all serve the same purpose: separation and identification.

Once a drug has been identified a number of questions arise. What is the significance of this? What bearing does the presence of the drug have on an investigation or court hearing? Could the drug have affected someone's behaviour? Did the accused person or the victim get into a fight because their inhibitions were reduced and their judgement impaired? The law takes a very straightforward position on this. Drunkenness or drug influenced behaviour are relevant to understanding and explaining events but neither negate culpability. Intoxication is not a defence in law because the possible consequences ought to have been foreseen. It is at best a mitigating factor.

Another important question is whether a drug could be implicated in the cause of death due to accident, suicide or murder. The concentration of the drug in the body provides a guide to its effect but this is influenced by many parameters and must be considered carefully. Dosage and individual tolerance can complicate interpretation. There have been instances where individuals have survived 'fatal' levels of a drug and other instances where a sub-fatal level has caused death. It is also common in death investigations to find more than one drug, sometimes several. Drug to drug interactions are a further complication. In some circumstances it is impossible to state what effect a cocktail of drugs would have had. In others, where different drugs have a similar pharmacological effect, this could be enhanced by the combination. For example, many benzodiazepines (e.g. Etizolam) and opioids (e.g. Methadone) cause respiratory depression as a side effect. Taken together this effect may be enhanced. Often a court wants to know the specific role that a drug played in a particular instance but it is rarely possible for this to be established scientifically.

In June 2014, Stephen Port phoned for an ambulance saying that a man appeared to have collapsed outside of his house in Barking, East London. The man, Anthony Walgate, was found to have died from GHB poisoning and had a bottle of GHB in his pocket. GHB use is most commonly associated with men who have sex with other men. Later the police found out that Port had hired Walgate as an escort. Port was charged and convicted of perverting the course of justice because he misled the police in his statement. In the course of the following year, the bodies of three other men were found propped against the churchyard walls of Barking Abbey (near where Port lived). In what has been called the 'Grindr' case (after the social networking app), the victims who died all had potentially fatal levels of GHB. In one instance GHB could not be stated as the sole cause of death because alcohol was also present. All of these men were killed by Port. He also attacked at least eight other men who survived, all of whom knew or strongly suspected that they had been surreptitiously drugged. Some of the men were raped, or sexually assaulted, others were unsure because they had been rendered unconscious (so could not have consented). None of them suspected Port at the outset. In one case, Port gave a 19-year-old university student a glass of red wine. When the student finished the wine, he noticed a congealed powder at the bottom of the glass and suspected the drink had been spiked. He then became disorientated, dizzy, and lost consciousness. In another case, the victim became unconscious almost immediately after drinking a soft drink given to him by Port. The victim was later seen by police at a railway station with Port. He was in a distressed and incoherent state, and was vomiting a green liquid. Port told the police the victim had taken 'G', the most common street name for GHB.

Port was convicted of the four murders as well as sexual offences and surreptitiously administering drugs to the eight other men. The Grindr case illustrates both the value and limitations of forensic toxicology. In the deaths, identifying GHB as a causal factor was due to the large concentrations found. In one of the other cases GHB was implicated by Port himself. However, the involvement of GHB (and possibly other drugs) in the remaining cases could only be inferred from witness accounts and circumstantial evidence because they did not come to notice until after Port was implicated in the murders. The important question that remains in this case is why the Metropolitan Police failed to connect these deaths despite their exceptionally unusual characteristics—a question that is still under investigation at time of writing.

Chapter 9
Science and justice—a case study

The defining feature of forensic science is its relationship with the law. In this chapter, we come to what are the final stages of a criminal inquiry—adjudication by the courts. This involves an encounter between science and law which raises many questions.

When a gun is fired, the hammer strikes the primer cap of the cartridge and the primer explodes, igniting the propellant. Hot gases from the propellant project the bullet from the cartridge case down the barrel of the gun. The gases escape from the barrel and other parts of the gun and condense to form GSR (see Chapter 4): microscopic particles composed of barium, antimony, and lead. The whole process takes about one-hundredth of a second. A gun being fired—any gun—is the only known source of GSR. A single shot produces tens of thousands of particles that land on the exposed skin or clothing of the person holding the gun and items nearby. The particles are easily transferred after they are deposited, so complicated and laborious anti-contamination procedures have to be carried out when recovering the residues.

In 1999, a man bundled Jill Dando, a TV personality and popular figure whose face was familiar to millions, to the ground, pressed a 9mm semi-automatic pistol against her left temple and fired a single shot. A 9mm cartridge and bullet were found on the doorstep at the scene.

A year later a man called Barry George was arrested. George's flat was searched and the police seized a coat that was hanging on his kitchen door. George agreed the coat was his. On forensic examination, a single particle of GSR was found inside a right inside pocket. The particle was identified by scanning electron microscopy and its composition established by X-ray analysis. The chemical elements in the particle were in the same proportion as the GSR particles in Dando's hair and on the cartridge found at the scene. The instrument and method of analysis are widely used in analytical science; the technology and methodology were well tested and reliable. GSR, traces of fibres and paints, shoe mark comparisons, fingerprint examinations, and all other forensic techniques are enabled by technology but made sense of by humans. The significance of the evidence is assessed by human cognition. The evidence is weighed carefully by experts but words can be misunderstood or manipulated. In a court of law, meaning is malleable in the hands of those sufficiently skilled and motivated. Argument is the business of law; sometimes the words can resist the force of these arguments, sometimes they cannot. Words do not speak on their own part; like the Bible they require exegesis. The expert witness is their interlocutor and the witness is as important as the words. A credible but untruthful witness may be believed while an anxious truthful one may not. A credulous witness can be exploited.

George was a fantasist and a liar. Police discovered a photograph of him posing with a replica gun wearing a gas mask and hood. He adopted false names, sometimes calling himself Paul Gadd (Gary Glitter's birth name) or Barry Bulsara, with its suggested link to Freddie Mercury, whose surname was Bulsara. He also concocted a false alibi. The GSR particle, together with eye-witness evidence and George's odd character, formed the basis of the prosecution case.

Orlando Pownall QC, one of the most successful and capable advocates in the country, was prosecution counsel. In his opening speech, Pownall stated that the GSR particle's similarity to those found on the body of Dando was 'compelling evidence' of George's guilt. A visual aid summarized this for the court. The message was simple, visual, almost subliminal, with only one possible conclusion: Barry George was guilty.

Michael Mansfield, another of the English Bar's most skilled and high-profile QCs, defended George. Mansfield is a formidable figure in court. He opened George's defence by suggesting that the murder had the hallmark features of a contract killing by a Serb. It was a 'precision shooting', with the gun placed against Dando's head to muffle the sound of the shot. There was some basis for this. Dando had made a TV appeal on behalf of Kosovan refugees which could have gained her Serbian enemies. Dando was also the anchor on *Crimewatch*, the BBC's flagship programme about unsolved high-profile police investigations. It was thought this may have made her some enemies as well. That the gun used to kill her was a conversion, a weapon that had been reactivated from a disabled one, weighed against this. No professional hit man would use this kind of gun, it was said.

Dr John Lloyd, an experienced expert witness, was called by the defence. He said it was 'incredible' that any significance could be put on a single GSR particle found a year after the incident. Lloyd also raised the spectre of contamination. When the police recover items for forensic examination they are packaged to preserve evidence and prevent contamination. The packaging should remain sealed until it is opened by a forensic scientist in the lab. But the police had removed the coat from its packaging to take photographs of it before passing it to the lab. Police officers who carried firearms were also said to use the same studio where the photographs were taken. Lloyd also suggested there could be other innocent means of contamination.

The single particle of GSR dominated the proceedings. The prosecution forensic expert, Robin Keeley, spent three days in the witness box dealing solely with potential contamination. One by one, he ruled out all the possibilities put to him by Mansfield, stating that each was 'remote'. Confusion crept into the debate and it became polarized. If the particle was due to contamination, it should be ruled out; if it wasn't due to contamination, the particle was evidence to link George to the murder. This reasoning was flawed. At the end of the trial, the jury deliberated for almost six days before convicting George by a majority verdict.

George appealed in 2002, challenging the identification evidence against him but the appeal was dismissed. He also made an application to the Criminal Cases Review Commission (CCRC), a body that reviews potential miscarriages of justice and has the power to refer them to the Court of Appeal for further consideration.

In January 2006, the FSS introduced new formal guidelines on the interpretation of single particles and low levels of GSR. Some believe this was coincidence, while others think there was a connection with the Dando case. The new guidelines recognized that finding GSR particles in the general population was rare, but the environmental level of GSR was now higher because firearms were being used more frequently in crime. There was a higher chance of innocent contamination than had been previously believed. Until then the undocumented practice had been to declare findings of very small amounts of residues, but state that they were of *no value*. Keeley did not comply with this.

In 2007, the CCRC referred the case back to the Court of Appeal. The change in FSS GSR reporting practice was one of several factors that raised doubts about the safety of the conviction. In the view of the CCRC, the prosecution had overplayed the significance of the GSR particle. The graphic produced by the police was also criticized; it left no room for interpretation. The report added that the defence, in trying to minimize the significance of the particle by focusing on contamination, missed the point. If the GSR particle was insignificant, as Lloyd had said in his evidence, it didn't matter how it had got on the coat. The CCRC were also critical of Keeley. His evidence did not convey to them that the particle was of no value. But they crucially added: 'the right question was never asked by anyone at trial'.

The Court of Appeal quashed Barry George's conviction in 2007. By this time George had been in prison for five years. They said that Keeley's evidence at the appeal (where he said the GSR particle was of no value) was different from that at the trial. There was no certainty that the jury would have come to the same decision if they had heard the appeal version. At the re-trial in 2008 the judge ruled the single particle of GSR inadmissible, and in the absence of other convincing evidence George was acquitted.

A single particle, one-hundredth of a millimetre in diameter, created in one-hundredth of a second in the flash of energy from a gun being fired, was debated for days and discombobulated almost everyone in court. The debate was pointless because the particle was of no significance so it didn't matter whether it was present due to contamination or not. The particle meant nothing; it had no value.

What went wrong here? Everything, you might respond: the prosecution overplayed the GSR evidence, the defence focused on contamination rather than the questionable significance of the single GSR particle; the expert witness attributed more significance to the particle than was warranted. Is this case typical? No, it is very unusual, but it gives a rare glimpse of how scientific evidence can be distorted in the heat of a high-profile adversarial trial. The murder of Jill Dando remains unsolved.

Concluding remarks

I have tried to provide the reader with some understanding of forensic science, its range, uses, and its limitations. Forensic science is not a single entity but an aggregation of disciplines, technologies, and practices that are applied to the questions that arise in criminal investigations and legal inquiries. Some elements of forensic science, such as DNA profiling, forensic toxicology, and analytical science more generally, are rooted in natural science. These have developed along scientific lines and will continue to do so. Other elements, such as fingerprint examination, rely more heavily on human agency than science and technology, and cannot develop in the same way. These disciplines are more susceptible to the human factors, such as prejudice and bias, that are inherently present. The canon of forensic technologies will continue to develop and change, in part due to the nature of the technologies themselves and in part due to the complex environment in which they are applied and the contingencies of the legal process. The conceptual gap between technology and the law is likely to remain—and perhaps increase.

References

Chapter 1: What is forensic science?

'The bloodstains looked like scattered fragments...' Alec Ross (2008). *The Rest is Noise: Listening to the Twentieth Century* (London: Fourth Estate).

Chapter 5: DNA profiling and databases

Amankwaa, A. O. (2018). 'Forensic DNA retention: Public perspective studies in the United Kingdom and around the world', *Science & Justice* 58: 455–64.

The Phantom of Heilbronn: https://www.theguardian.com/lifeand-style/2008/nov/09/germany-serial-killer (retrieved 27 June 2019).

Chapter 6: Prints and marks: more ways to identify people and things

Evett, I. W., and Williams, R. L. (1996). 'Review of the sixteen points fingerprint standard in England and Wales', *Journal of Forensic Identification* 46(1): 49–73.

Chapter 8: Drugs and toxicology

The United Kingdom Drug Situation (2017). *United Kingdom Focal Point* (London: Public Health England).

Fiorentin, T. R., and Logan, B. K. (2019). 'Toxicological findings in 1000 cases of suspected drug facilitated sexual assault in the

United States', *Journal of Forensic and Legal Medicine* 61 (February).

'...there is little scientific knowledge about the long-term effects cannabis use...' National Academies of Health and Medicine (2017). 'The health effects of cannabis and cannabinoids: The current state of evidence and recommendations for research', http://nationalacademies.org/hmd/reports/2017/health-effects-of-cannabis-and-cannabinoids.aspx (retrieved 10 July 2019).

Chapter 9: Science and justice—a case study

The quotations from the CCRC report in the George case are from an article published in the *Daily Mail*: https://www.dailymail.co.uk/news/article-463975/Revealed-The-100-page-report-set-Jill-Dando-killer-free.html (retrieved 21 February 2019).

Further reading

The forensic ecosystem

Fraser, J., and Williams, R. (eds.) (2009). *The Handbook of Forensic Science* (London: Routledge). An edited volume which covers all of the areas in this book as well as social, legal, economic, and political aspects of forensic science. A little out of date in the more technical chapters now but still relevant in many other aspects.

National Academy of Sciences (2009). *Strengthening Forensic Science in the United States: A Path Forward* (Washington, DC: The National Academies). Available online at: https://www.nap.edu/catalog/12589/strengthening-forensic-science-in-the-united-states-a-path-forward (retrieved 29 June 2019).

Her Majesty's Inspector of Constabulary (2002). 'Under the microscope refocused: A revisit to an earlier thematic inspection report on scientific and technical support'. The first report is not readily available but this report contains a summary of the original findings and further confirms them as ongoing issues. Available online at: https://www.justiceinspectorates.gov.uk/hmicfrs/media/under-the-microscope-20020601.pdf (retrieved 2 February 2019).

Crime investigation

Stelfox, P. (2009). *Criminal Investigation: An Introduction to Principles and Practice* (Cullompton: Willan). An excellent overview of how major criminal investigations operate.

Crime scene investigation

Tilstone, W. J., et al. (2013). *Fisher's Techniques of Crime Scene Investigation*, First International Edition (London: CRC Press). A detailed introduction by subject experts with an investigative focus and many case examples.

Work in the laboratory

White, P. (ed.) (2016). *Crime Scene to Court: The Essentials of Forensic Science*, Fourth Edition (London: Royal Society of Chemistry). Covers all of the scientific areas in this book and more.

Bell, S. (2013). *Forensic Chemistry*, New International Edition (Harlow: Pearson). A detailed technical introduction to the topic.

DNA profiling and databases

Sense about Science (2017). *Making Sense of Forensic Genetics* (London: Sense about Science). A short and very accessible overview for the general reader available at: https://senseaboutscience.org/activities/making-sense-of-forensic-genetics/ (retrieved January 2019).

Butler, J. M. (2012). *Advanced Topics in Forensic DNA Typing: Methodology* (San Diego, CA: Elsevier Academic Press). The standard DNA reference text; requires significant technical knowledge of the subject.

Index

For the benefit of digital users, indexed terms that span two pages (e.g., 52–53) may, on occasion, appear on only one of those pages.

A

acid phosphatase (AP)
  test 39–40
alcohol 33, 93, 99
  analysis 26, 101
  back calculation 101
  breathalyser 100–1
  drink-driving 26, 99–100
  drink-driving limits 99–100
  pharmacology 99
  risk of fatal crash 100

B

back calculation, *see* alcohol
Bayes, Reverend Thomas (Bayesian
  reasoning) 61–2
bias 36, 59, 60, 76, 112
Birmingham Six 9–10
Black, Robert 90
blood 38–41
  bloodstain pattern analysis
    (BPA) 25–30
  identification 38–9
  Kastle Meyer (KM) bloodstain
    test 38–9

body fluids 24, 38–41, 59, 63
  analytical methods 42
  presumptive tests 38–40, 42
  saliva 40, 42
  semen 26, 36, 38–42, 46
  sexual offences, body fluids
    in 26, 38, 40
breathalyser, *see* alcohol

C

cannabis, *see* illicit drugs
cartridge casing, striations 25–7,
  66
CCTV 8–9, 12–13, 34
  in crime investigation 13
  in Suzanne Pilley case 11–12
  see also digital forensics
chromatographic methods 42
  gas chromatography 42, 101
  gas-liquid
    chromatography 103–4
  pyrolysis gas chromatography-
    mass spectrometry 92
  thin layer chromatography
    (TLC) 87
classification vs identification 5–6

cocaine, *see* illicit drugs
confirmation bias *see* bias
contamination 19, 20, 30, 31, 35, 36, 54, 81, 109–11
    of crime scene 18–19
    in DNA analysis (prevention of) 52–3
    in Jill Dando case 109–11
    in laboratory 31, 92
    Phantom of Heilbronn 53–4
    in Rachel Nickell case 41
Criminal Cases Review Commission (CCRC) 110–11
crime scene, *see* crime scene management
crime scene investigator (CSI) 18, 20
crime scene management 17–19
    cordons 18–19
    labelling/packaging items 20
    preservation 18–19
    recording 19
    recovery of evidence 19
crime scene manager (CSM) 18, 20
crime types, and forensic evidence 26
criminal law, *see* law

D

Dando, Jill 108
date rape, *see* drug facilitated sexual assault (DFSA), 102
digital forensics 13–14
    cell site analysis 12–15
    CCTV 8–9, 12–13, 34
    data extraction 13–14
    desktop computers 34
    encrypted data 13–14
    IMEI number 12
    metadata 12
    mobile phones 12–14
    social media 13
DNA
    analysis 49–54
    contamination 52–3

databases 62–3
differential extraction 50–2
DNA 17, DNA 24 50–2
electropherograms (EPG) 54–7
evaluating evidence 59–61
extraction and purification 49–50
genotype frequencies 60
kinship testing 55
massive parallel sequencing (MPS) 64
mitochondrial 47–8
mixture interpretation 58–9
next generation sequencing (NGS) 64
polymerase chain reaction (PCR) 51
short tandem repeats (STRs) 49
structure of DNA 48
Y-STR 62–3
drink-driving, *see* alcohol
drugs *see also* illicit drugs
    analysis and analytical methods 103–6
    definition 93
    dosage 104–5
    half-life 102–3
    interactions 104–5
    possession 94–5
    tolerance 93–4, 104–5
    trafficking and supply 26, 94
drug facilitated sexual assault (DFSA) 102
    Stephen Port case 105–6

E

ecstasy, *see* illicit drugs
expert evidence 109–10

F

fibres 82–90
    comparison with control sample 85–7
    comparison microscope 85–7

evaluation of evidence 88
Fourier Transform Infrared
    Spectroscopy 42, 87, 92
identification 85–7
loss from skin and other
    surfaces 3
microspectrophotometry 42, 86
tapings 83–5
target fibre 84
thin layer chromatography
    (TLC) 42, 85–7, 92
transfer 4–5, 88
fingerprints 68–9
    automatic fingerprint
        identification systems
        (AFIS) 69–70
    comparison with marks 73–4
    confirmation bias 75–6
    identification standards 75–8
    miscarriages of justice,
        see McKie, Shirley; Mayfield,
        Brandon
    national fingerprint database in
        UK (IDENT1) 68
    prints vs marks 70
    recovery of latent marks 73
    ridge patterns 71
firearms 25–7, 42
    GSR 107–11
    marks on cartridges 66
footwear (and shoe
    marks) 78–80
forensic science defined 6–7
forensic strategy 22–4
Fourier Transform Infrared
    Spectroscopy (FTIR) 42, 87, 92

G

Galton, Francis 69
George, Barry 108
GHB (gamma hydroxybutyrate), see
    illicit drugs
glass 26, 42, 81
gunshot residues (GSR) 107–10

H

Hampton, Christopher 46
heroin, see illicit drugs
Home Office Large Major Enquiry
    System (HOLMES computer
    system) 9, 11

I

IDENT1, national fingerprint
    database in UK 68
illicit drugs
    benzodiazepines 93, 95–6,
        103–5
    cathiniones 95–6
    classification, Classes A, B,
        and C 94–5
    cocaine 94–5
    ecstasy 95–6
    fentanyl 93
    gammahydroxybutyrate
        (GHB) 95–6, 102–3, 105–6
    hashish 96–7
    heroin 98
    mephedrone 95–6
    new psychoactive substances
        (NPS) 95–6
    possession of 94
    tetrahydrocannabinol (THC)
    trafficking and supply 26, 94
    see also drugs
individualization 6

J

Jeffreys, Sir Alec 47

K

Kastle-Meyer (KM) bloodstain
    test 38–9
kinship testing, DNA
    profiling 55
Kirk, Paul 1–3, 6, 61

L

laboratories
  disciplines, departments, and
    case types 33
  examination of items 36–8
law
  mens rea and *actus reus* 8–9
  miscarriage of justice
    9–10, 110
  Misuse of Drugs Act 1971
    UK 94–5
  Misuse of Drugs Regulations
    2001 UK 94–5
  Psychoactive Substances Act
    2016 95–6
legal highs, *see* new psychoactive
  substances (NPS)
Locard, Edmond, principles of
  forensic science 1–3, 5

M

McKie, Shirley 76–7
Madrid bombings 77
Mann, Klaus 1
marks
  cartridge casing, striations 66
  confirmation bias 75–6
  enhancement 78–9
  evaluation of 78–9
  lasers and ultraviolet
    light 73
  latent 65–6, 73
  recovery of marks 73
  see also fingerprints; shoe marks
Mayfield, Brandon 77
mobile phones, *see* digital
  forensics

N

new psychoactive substances
  (NPS) 95–6
Nickell, Rachel 36, 92

P

packaging of forensic
  evidence 20
Pilley, Suzanne 11
paint 90–2
  in Rachel Nickell case 92
Phantom of Heilbronn 53–4
physical fits 41–5
polymerase chain reaction 51
Port, Stephen 105–6
prints, *see* fingerprints
Psychoactive Substances Act
  (2016) 95–6
Pulp Fiction and hypothesis
  testing 21–2

R

Road, Melanie 46
Ross, Marion 76–7

S

senior investigating officer (SIO),
  role 9
shoe marks
  case example, Peter
    Voisey 30
  comparison 79
  latent, visualization 78–9
  pattern and manufacturing
    features 78–9
Stone, Michael 6, 29–30

T

trace evidence 20, 24, 25, 35, 37,
  42, 81–92
  transfer and persistence
    3–4, 82
  see also Wright, Steve
trace, interview, eliminate (TIE)
  approach 9–10
toxicology 98–102

analytical methods 103
case example, Stephen
  Port 105–6
death investigation 104–5
drug interactions 104–5
interpretation of
  results 103–6

V

Voisey, Peter 79–80

W

Wright, Steve 88–9

RACISM
A Very Short Introduction
Ali Rattansi

From subtle discrimination in everyday life and scandals in politics, to incidents like lynchings in the American South, cultural imperialism, and 'ethnic cleansing', racism exists in many different forms, in almost every facet of society. But what actually is race? How has racism come to be so firmly established? Why do so few people actually admit to being racist? How are race, ethnicity, and xenophobia related? This book reincorporates the latest research to demystify the subject of racism and explore its history, science, and culture. It sheds light not only on how racism has evolved since its earliest beginnings, but will also explore the numerous embodiments of racism, highlighting the paradox of its survival, despite the scientific discrediting of the notion of 'race' with the latest advances in genetics.

www.oup.com/vsi

FORENSIC PSYCHOLOGY

A Very Short Introduction

David Canter

Lie detection, offender profiling, jury selection, insanity in the law, predicting the risk of re-offending, the minds of serial killers and many other topics that fill news and fiction are all aspects of the rapidly developing area of scientific psychology broadly known as Forensic Psychology. *Forensic Psychology: A Very Short Introduction* discusses all the aspects of psychology that are relevant to the legal and criminal process as a whole. It includes explanations of criminal behaviour and criminality, including the role of mental disorder in crime, and discusses how forensic psychology contributes to helping investigate the crime and catching the perpetrators.

www.oup.com/vsi

HIV/AIDS
A Very Short Introduction
Alan Whiteside

HIV/AIDS is without doubt the worst epidemic to hit humankind since the Black Death. The first case was identified in 1981; by 2004 it was estimated that about 40 million people were living with the disease, and about 20 million had died. The news is not all bleak though. There have been unprecedented breakthroughs in understanding diseases and developing drugs. Because the disease is so closely linked to sexual activity and drug use, the need to understand and change behaviour has caused us to reassess what it means to be human and how we should operate in the globalising world. This *Very Short Introduction* provides an introduction to the disease, tackling the science, the international and local politics, the fascinating demographics, and the devastating consequences of the disease, and explores how we have — and must — respond.

'It won't make you an expert. But you'll know what you're talking about and you'll have a better idea of all the work we still have to do to wrestle this monster to the ground.'

Aids-free world website.

www.oup.com/vsi

NUCLEAR POWER
A Very Short Introduction
Maxwell Irvine

The term 'nuclear power' causes anxiety in many people and there is confusion concerning the nature and extent of the associated risks. Here, Maxwell Irvine presents a concise introduction to the development of nuclear physics leading up to the emergence of the nuclear power industry. He discusses the nature of nuclear energy and deals with various aspects of public concern, considering the risks of nuclear safety, the cost of its development, and waste disposal. Dispelling some of the widespread confusion about nuclear energy, Irvine considers the relevance of nuclear power, the potential of nuclear fusion, and encourages informed debate about its potential.

www.oup.com/vsi

PLANETS
A Very Short Introduction
David A. Rothery

This *Very Short Introduction* looks deep into space and describes the worlds that make up our Solar System: terrestrial planets, giant planets, dwarf planets and various other objects such as satellites (moons), asteroids and Trans-Neptunian objects. It considers how our knowledge has advanced over the centuries, and how it has expanded at a growing rate in recent years. David A. Rothery gives an overview of the origin, nature, and evolution of our Solar System, including the controversial issues of what qualifies as a planet, and what conditions are required for a planetary body to be habitable by life. He looks at rocky planets and the Moon, giant planets and their satellites, and how the surfaces have been sculpted by geology, weather, and impacts.

"The writing style is exceptionally clear and pricise"

Astronomy Now

Scientific Revolution
A Very Short Introduction
Lawrence M. Principe

In this *Very Short Introduction* Lawrence M. Principe explores the exciting developments in the sciences of the stars (astronomy, astrology, and cosmology), the sciences of earth (geography, geology, hydraulics, pneumatics), the sciences of matter and motion (alchemy, chemistry, kinematics, physics), the sciences of life (medicine, anatomy, biology, zoology), and much more. The story is told from the perspective of the historical characters themselves, emphasizing their background, context, reasoning, and motivations, and dispelling well-worn myths about the history of science.

www.oup.com/vsi

GEOPOLITICS
A Very Short Introduction
Klaus Dodds

In certain places such as Iraq or Lebanon, moving a few feet either side of a territorial boundary can be a matter of life or death, dramatically highlighting the connections between place and politics. For a country's location and size as well as its sovereignty and resources all affect how the people that live there understand and interact with the wider world. Using wide-ranging examples, from historical maps to James Bond films and the rhetoric of political leaders like Churchill and George W. Bush, this Very Short Introduction shows why, for a full understanding of contemporary global politics, it is not just smart - it is essential - to be geopolitical.

'Engrossing study of a complex topic.'

Mick Herron, Geographical.

www.oup.com/vsi